HEARTS AT WAR

1914-19

The author laying a wreath on behalf of the Scottish Football Association at Contalmaison, 1 July 2014.

HEARTS AT WAR

1914-19

Tom Purdie

First published 2014

Amberley Publishing
The Hill, Stroud
Gloucestershire, GL5 4EP

www.amberley-books.com

British Library Cataloguing in Publication Data.
A catalogue record for this book is available from the British Library.

ISBN 978 1 4456 3320 6 (print)
ISBN 978 1 4456 3334 3 (ebook)

Typeset in 10.5pt on 14pt Sabon.
Typesetting and Origination by Amberley Publishing.
Printed in the UK.

Contents

	Author's Note	7
	Acknowledgements	9
	Foreword by John Robertson	11
	Introduction	13
1	The Summer of 1914	21
2	Season 1915/16	61
3	The Somme, 1916	81
4	Season 1916/17	99
5	Season 1917/18	113
6	Season 1918/19	125
7	1919 and Beyond	137
	Notes	155

Author's Note

This book is dedicated to the followers and players of Heart of Midlothian who served their country and died in the Great War of 1914–19, and equally to their comrades who served and lived to return; and also to the people who remained at home who, with unstinting effort and sacrifice, helped to bring the club through that extremely trying and difficult time in its proud history.

Acknowledgements

I would like to express my thanks to the following for their assistance in the making of this book: Firstly, Heart of Midlothian Football Club for allowing me access to the Minute Books pertaining to the 1914–19 period and to their small, but magnificent, collection and extremely valuable club memorabilia from that era, the Scottish Premier Football League, Neil Anderson, James Findlay, Craig Herbertson, Stewart Ryce, Margaret Strickland, Iain Manson, Tom Logan, Bob Craig, Marshall Bowman, London Hearts website, Third Lanark historian Bob Laird and Scott Struthers, club secretary of Hamilton Academical.

Special thanks are due to Jack Alexander, the author of the excellent *McCrae's Battalion*, which told the full story of the Hearts enlistment for the first time and inspired the overdue construction of the Contalmaison Cairn in France.

In the early days of the formation of the book I was fortunate to recieve advice from a noted historian of the Scottish game, Heart of Midlothian's historian, David Speed, who also assisted me greatly in the preparation and guidance and gave his time generously.

I would like to extend my appreciation to a very good friend, Heart of Midlothian legend John Robertson, for taking the time to present an excellent foreword. John's love of everything connected with Heart of Midlothian knows no bounds.

I would never have written this book had it not been for Louis Archard of Amberley Publishing approaching, me and his encouragement was greatly appreciated.

One of the greatest bonuses for the author in writing this book was to gain a better understanding of not just how football was in Scotland 100 years ago, but the hardships and tribulations the people of this nation had to bear during the Great War. It was a humbling experience to look back to those days from 1914 to 1919 and learn of the sacrifices made by many, not only in the field of battle but on the home front.

Football was virtually all that the working classes had left and it was a welcome distraction from the drudgery of life; if they had been deprived of this outlet then they would have had almost nothing.

The Heart of Midlothian Football Club ensured that they were there for the people and the people ensured that they were there for the Heart of Midlothian Football Club.

Foreword by John Robertson

As I sat in the office of Heart of Midlothian's Chief Executive, David Southern, the request was quite simple but ultimately stark and chilling.

Sergius Fedetovas, Vladimir Romanov's right-hand man, went straight to the point. 'If we do not raise just short of two million pounds, the club will go into administration and subsequent liquidation.'

I was stunned. Not by the possibility of the club being in financial trouble – this had been forecast by many for a long time now as the majority shareholder's companies had suffered huge losses and the spending on wages over previous seasons was not sustainable for a club with the turnover of Hearts – but to hear the amount that was required in such a short space of time.

What followed over the coming months was remarkable as Hearts fans rallied round their club and showed that it was much more than a football institution to them. It was described in many quarters as a 'call to arms'.

As media proclamations go, it was a sensationalised headline that made clear of the need for the club's players, fans and everyone connected to Heart of Midlothian to come forward and do their bit to help the famous old club survive.

While it was not a time that any Hearts fan wanted to experience, the response was, as I previously said, quite incredible... However, history shows that we should have not have been too surprised. This was not the first time the 'Hearts Family' had come to the fore, and while I would gladly shake every single person by the hand who helped keep Hearts alive during those long winter months to allow a potential and healthier future, these efforts pale in significance to the events of exactly 100 years ago.

You are about to read about young men who rallied to the cause for king and country when they were needed most, the great majority of whom joined under the charismatic leadership of Sir George McCrae. Sir George raised a battalion of over 1,100 men in a matter of months to be ready for deployment on the front line. You are about to read about the Hearts men who chose to join other regiments in the fight against the foe.

How a Hearts team in their prime, and with all the qualities required to win the League title in season 1914/15, lost out to the eventual winners, Celtic.

How the players mixed their football duties with their Army training and signed up to the new battalion, followed by players from seventy-five senior and junior teams and over 600 of their own supporters as they prepared to face the most brutal and horrible of all wars ever fought.

The Great War will always be synonymous with Heart of Midlothian and will always be part of the club's historical fabric. While thousands of fans kept the club alive in 2013/14, read now about those that went before, those who did what no one could have asked of them, those who made the sacrifices for this great and glorious club. I am delighted to be chosen to write the foreword for this book.

John Robertson
Hearts FC and Scotland

Introduction

I remember it clearly. It was a beautiful summer's afternoon in mid-June and I was sitting in the garden at home, enjoying the warm sunshine and at peace with the world. Suddenly my mobile phone began to ring and, on answering, I learned that the caller was none other than Gary Ralston, a sports journalist with the *Daily Record* whom I have known for a good number of years. Gary was calling from Tynecastle and the breaking news he gave me was not good. Hearts had just gone into administration. The warm air suddenly had a chill to it as I thanked Gary for taking the time to call me. I sat very quiet for a while, deep in thought as to the ramifications of the news for this famous old club steeped in history, and the challenges that lay ahead.

Earlier in the year, the fans of Hearts had answered a rallying call by one of their favourite sons, John Robertson, who, acting on behalf of the club, asked them to rescue Hearts from financial disaster and to help save the club from going 'to the wall'. The response was immediate as the support gave what they had, some their life savings, to raise almost £2 million through a share issue. But their efforts had been in vain. Going indoors, I turned on the television in time to hear a newsreader describing the situation at Hearts as the blackest time in the club's history. The situation was dire – of that there was no doubt – but I didn't consider it the blackest time in the history of Heart of Midlothian. My thoughts took me back in time to 1914, at the outbreak of the Great War, when almost an entire football team decided to enlist in the British Army and fight for king and country. They traded the playing fields of Scotland for the killing fields of France. They traded the roar of the crowd for the roar of gunfire. The players were of the view that their contract was not with their club but their country and gave up their footballer's pay of £4 per week to take the king's shilling – a shilling a day was their wage. They had played together, and now they were to fight together and ultimately die together in what was to become known as 'the Supreme Sacrifice', a reminder to us all that life is as delicate as it is precious.

On 1 July 1916, a date which will remain forever in the hearts of the maroon faithful, the side was decimated at the Battle of the Somme. The Somme – a small corner of France that will forever be Tynecastle. The men who voluntarily went to Belgium and France encapsulated Heart of Midlothian Football Club.

THE HEART OF MIDLOTHIAN FC PLAYERS ROLL OF HONOUR

Private James Speedie, 7th Cameron Highlanders	Killed in action 25 September 1915
Corporal Thomas Gracie, 16th Royal Scots	Died in service 23 October 1915
Sergeant Duncan Currie, 16th Royal Scots	Killed in action 1 July 1916
Private Ernest Ellis, 16th Royal Scots	Killed in action 1 July 1916
Private Henry Wattie, 16th Royal Scots	Killed in action 1 July 1916
L/Corporal James Boyd, 16th Royal Scots	Killed in action 3 August 1916
Sergeant John Allan, 9th Royal Scots	Killed in action 22 April 1917

*

Gunner Colin Blackhall, RGA 1st Lowland	
Corporal Alfred Briggs, 16th Royal Scots	Severely wounded
Private Patrick Crossan, 16th Royal Scots	Twice wounded and gassed
Corporal Norman Findlay, 16th Royal Scots	
Sergeant James Frew, 16th Royal Scots and RGA 1st Lowland	
Bombardier James Gilbert, RGA 1st Lowland	
Private Harry Graham, Gloucester Regiment and RAMC	
Sapper Charles Hallwood, Royal Engineers	
Private James Hazeldean, 16th Royal Scots	Twice wounded
Lt James Low, 16th Royal Scots and 6th Seaforth Highlanders	Twice wounded
L/Corporal James Macdonald, 13th Royal Scots	
Private Edward McGuire, 18th Royal Scots	Wounded
Gunner John Mackenzie, RGA 1st Lowland	
Private James Martin, 5th Royal Scots	Wounded
Bombardier Robert Mercer, RGA 1st Lowland	Severely gassed
Sergeant George Miller, 9th Royal Scots	
Sergeant Neil Moreland, 8th HLI and 7th Royal Scots	Twice wounded

Lieut. Annan Ness, 16th Royal Scots and 9th Royal Scots	Twice wounded
Private Robert Preston, 18th Royal Scots	Wounded
Driver George Sinclair, Royal Field Artillery	Injured and discharged
Private Philip Whyte, Gloucester Regiment	
Private John Wilson, 9th Royal Scots	Twice wounded
L/Corporal William Wilson, 18th and 16th Royal Scots	Wounded

No war is kind but the First World War was brutal in the extreme. It was devastating for everyone involved. Young men were sent to a war that many thought would be over by Christmas, but within a short space of time it turned into a vision of hell, with trenches and wire running across the battlefields of Flanders, Loos, Ypres, Mons and the Somme. Young boys, some of them only fifteen and sixteen years of age, who had barely travelled beyond their own city, town or village, watched as their friends and comrades were either blown up, shot or gassed. Killed in front of their eyes. In a war of attrition, millions died or were wounded in appalling conditions. A whole generation of men went to their deaths in the trenches.

My maternal grandfather, Tom Findlay, had been called up at the start of the Great War. Having served in the Boer War, he was classed as an Army reservist and was part of the British Expeditionary Force to be sent to France. He had fought at the Battle of Mons, which opened at daybreak on 23 August 1914, at Le Cateau and on the Marne. My grandfather loved to recount to me, as a young boy, stories of the two wars he had fought in and he often told me about the Angel of Mons and truly believed in what thousands of men had seen in the sky above the battlefield. This was the legendary tale of the wounded and dying British soldiers on the Mons battlefield who saw strange angelic forms in the sky that protected them from slaughter by the Germans. Some sceptics dismissed it as myth but many veterans of the war continued to believe in the Angel of Mons for the rest of their lives and my grandfather was one of them. The story of the Angel of Mons lives on today in folklore and legend.

I would sit by the fireside, listening intently to him as he regaled me with his many tales. Sometimes he would stop to relight his pipe between stories and gaze wistfully into the coal fire burning away merrily in the fireplace. It was as if he was being transported back in time, reliving the moment, and occasionally there was a certain sadness on his face before he continued where he had left off. But he rarely spoke about the horrors of the Great War, preferring to tell light-hearted stories about his comrades' exploits, and for my benefit he would make it all sound like a great adventure. Only in later years did I learn the full story. By way of books, radio, television and first-hand accounts, I gleaned knowledge of the carnage, the mayhem, the death, the destruction, the suffering and the absolute terror which he had witnessed. Only then did I realise my grandfather's reluctance to tell the true version of the events that had taken place all those years ago. But his generation, many of whom witnessed scenes of horror that the generation of today can hardly imagine, believed in reticence and chose to keep their nightmares to themselves.

I had visited some of the battlefields of the Great War over the years and had never failed to be touched and saddened when seeing row upon row of the headstones of those who had fallen, in the lovingly and carefully tended cemeteries. The memory of my first ever visit to the Somme will remain with me forever. As I stood looking out over the pleasant, rolling green fields, which were bathed in sunshine, with the only sounds being the singing of the birds, I found it difficult to comprehend the horror and death that had taken place here when the sounds heard were of the dying and wounded interspersed with the ear-splitting sounds of shelling and the rattle of machine guns. I found it difficult to imagine that these pleasant, rolling green fields which lay before me were once trenches where the soldiers spent their time in miserable and bleak conditions which were practically indescribable.

Since the battle, the fields have been ploughed and sown every year and the plough still brings up shells. Depending on the time of year, distinct white lines reveal where the trenches had been dug into the chalk beneath. There are other silent reminders of 1 July 1916, the Lochnager mine crater being the most obvious.

As I continued to gaze over the land the lyrics of that haunting song 'The Green Fields of France', written by Eric Bogle, came to mind:

> The sun now it shines on the green fields of France
> There's a warm summer breeze it makes the red poppies dance
> And look how the sun shines from under the clouds
> There's no gas, no barbed wire, there's no gun firing now.

This was the place where the majority of the Hearts players and supporters had fallen. This was the place – a small corner of France – that will forever be Tynecastle.

The Gordon Dump Cemetery on the Somme is one which is particularly moving. The vast number of the men commemorated there fell in action during the fighting which took place in July 1916. Almost two-thirds of the soldiers who lie buried there are unidentified, the only inscription on the headstones being 'A Soldier of the Great War, Known unto God'.

Heart of Midlothian had been part of those events. Was all this history going to disappear along with the name Heart of Midlothian Football Club? A name which sets it apart from any other footballing side in the country, a name which is quite simply unique.

Hearts have always been a credit to the game ever since their story began. It has been a story of great achievements and times of tragedy but it has never been a story without interest or romance, going back to the days of a handful of young men kicking a ball about in the Meadows in 1873.

My phone once again came to life and I answered, fully expecting it to be someone wishing to discuss Hearts' plight. But I was wrong. It was Louis Archard from Amberley Publishing, asking me if I would be willing to write a book about the part that Heart of Midlothian had played in the Great War. It didn't take a lot of time for me to say 'yes'. Was it coincidence that I received the call hard on the heels of the one from Gary Ralston? I think it was fate. I had already written a book published by Amberley called *Hearts: The Golden Years* a few months previously which reflected on the club's most successful period in history during the years 1954 to 1963, and in the tome I had alluded to Heart of Midlothian's involvement in the Great War. Now I was being given the opportunity to recount the tale of the bravest group of sportsmen Scotland had ever known, the lads who fell in the morning of their days with the dew of health upon their brows. Also, I was being given the chance to describe, in as much detail as possible, the events of the season of 1914/15, which led to Hearts losing the League championship, and to let a younger generation understand how it all materialised as a League title was cruelly torn from their grasp in the last few weeks of the season. But most importantly, it was to give them a better understanding as to why Heart of Midlothian were admired by the nation almost 100 years ago and to this day are revered the world over.

But it wasn't just the players who had made the sacrifice; the supporters joined up as well to serve with the men they had once watched and cheered on from the terraces at Tynecastle. The ones left behind also made sacrifices. The people behind the scenes at Tynecastle who kept the club going during the dark years. Hearts had dedicated staff, in particular the manager, John McCartney, who worked all hours for the club, Jimmy Duckworth the trainer, his assistant Alex Lyon and the groundsman, Tom Murphy. The young players who had to try and fill the boots of the senior players who were overseas. The families, the wives, the girlfriends and, of course, those ordinary supporters who toiled in the important home industries, becoming part of the war machine, but always gave to the club's fundraising activities for those in service. The ones who continued to support the club by finding time to attend as many games as they could during those troubled times.

Finally, there was the Board of Directors, who all had specific tasks to carry out at the club and are more than worthy of mention. Possibly no set of directors in the game had a more trying and stressful time during the dreary war years than those holding office at Tynecastle.

William Drummond was a shareholder from 1905. He was a clerk who lived at Shandon in Edinburgh. Drummond was elected to the Board in March 1909 and he served on the Finance Sub-Committee from 1909 to 1920. He played a major part in arranging finance for the building of the Main Stand and was, of course, one of the directors who decided that no obstacle would be placed in the way of the players joining the Army. Drummond helped to successfully conduct the club through the Great War and then, in March 1920, after sterling service, he did not seek re-election. William Drummond played his part in Heart of Midlothian being free of debt, despite the cost of the Main Stand soaring from £8,000 to £12,178 and with all the stress of the war.

William Brown was a builder and his company, based in the south side of Edinburgh, often worked on Hearts' stadium. In 1905 he bought five shares and regularly increased his holding. Brown was elected to the Board in 1910 and, not surprisingly, he served on the Ground Committee for many years. He also had a good knowledge of football, and in 1911 took charge of the 'A' team. Brown was instrumental in the club's first overseas tours in 1912 and 1914 and in the building of the Main Stand in 1914. He also gave his full support to the players who wished to enlist and thereafter helped to keep Hearts operating under financial pressure during the war years. His firm regularly undertook metalwork and plumbing for Hearts and he loaned the club funds on more than one occasion. William Brown was regularly re-elected and little did he know that he would serve Heart of Midlothian through another world war before he retired from the Board in June 1945.

William Lorimer became a member of Hearts when the club moved to Gorgie in 1881. He was a maker of Venetian blinds in Powderhall and was actually president when Hearts won the Scottish Cup in 1896. Lorimer then became a shareholder in the 1903 company and was a subscriber to the 1905 company. This was formed to take over the assets and liabilities of the old concern. Lorimer was appointed chairman in July 1905, at the initial board meeting. He stepped down in 1906, but remained on the board. A born diplomat and an excellent judge of a player, Lorimer was elected President of the Scottish Football Association for 1909–10 and also served on various SFA boards, including the International Selection Committee. Lorimer was fully supportive of the players' decision to enlist and tragically lost his own son during the fighting in France. In March 1922 he decided to retire and received from the SFA a cheque for £100 in recognition of his long and valuable service. The club awarded him a gold medal and life membership to mark twenty-eight years' service. William Lorimer died in Edinburgh on 4 March 1939 at the grand old age of ninety years.

William Burns, a Hearts supporter since 1887, was invited to join the Board of Directors in August 1906. Burns was a prominent official in the financial branch of Edinburgh Corporation Education Department. Naturally, he served on Hearts' Finance Sub-Committee from March 1907 and was appointed Honorary Treasurer in June that year. Burns also played his part in the development of the new stand and his diligent work through the dark times of the war helped keep the club going. He was behind the players when the decision to enlist was made. William Burns carried out many tasks in the name of Heart of Midlothian and served as chairman from 1922 to 1924. He eventually retired in March 1941 but remained an active shareholder until his death in August 1949.

And finally the chairman, Elias Henry Furst, who was born in Russia in 1873. His father Jacob became minister of the Edinburgh Hebrew Congregation after the family moved to Scotland. Elias became a watchmaker and jeweller in South Bridge, Edinburgh, and developed into an astute businessman. He was appointed one of the club's auditors at the turn of the century and was never shy in challenging the Club Committee over matters he didn't agree with. In 1905 he was instrumental in assisting with restructuring the business and two years later was invited onto the Board with responsibility for finance and ground development. Furst was made vice-chairman in September 1909 and backed the appointment of John McCartney as manager to replace the unpopular and unsuccessful James McGhee. In March 1912, at the age of thirty-nine, he became chairman and thus the real driving force behind the building of the Main Stand. Thereafter, Elias Furst steered the club through difficult financial years and kept the people at Hearts working together despite the never-ending bad news arriving from the front line on what seemed to be a regular basis. He was a man of strong character who loved the club with a passion but eventually the hard work and the long hours began to affect his health. In later years Furst, who was becoming tired of the infighting that was taking place at Hearts, stood down from the Board in 1935 after some friction about the possible selling of their star player at that time, Tommy Walker. Elias Furst remained a shareholder until he passed away in June 1949.

These were the people from the 'Hearts Family' who had all played their part in helping to bring the club through the blackest period in the Gorgie side's history.

I felt honoured yet humble to be able to recount a tale of courage, bravery, sacrifice, sadness, compassion with the occasional piece of good fortune, and suddenly the gloom lifted.

This is their story.

1

The Summer of 1914

At the end of the 1913/14 season, Hearts had finished in third place in the League with a then club record of fifty-four points. The fans were certainly supportive and attendances had hit a new peak, with a League average of 13,000. Hopes were high down Gorgie way for the coming League campaign and manager John McCartney was confident that his side could win the championship. Since McCartney's arrival at Hearts in January 1910, the team had developed well under his guidance and was now poised and ready to take the title from the reigning champions, Celtic. He knew this would be no easy task but in the squad McCartney had pieced together there were players with the qualities to achieve this. Players such as Archie Boyd, James Speedie, Annan Ness, James Boyd, Harry Wattie, Tom Gracie, Paddy Crossan, Duncan Currie, Alfie Briggs, Jimmy Low, Harry Graham, Willie Wilson, George Sinclair and, of course, his captain, Bob Mercer. During the close season Hearts undertook a second overseas tour, the first one being two years earlier, and recorded a famous 2-1 victory over the Danish international side. The Hearts squad was thought to be one of its finest in the history of the club, although the players' exploits off the field would eventually earn more fame.

A main grandstand, designed by the renowned architect Archibald Leitch, was also under construction at this time. In February 1914, Leitch had submitted his plans and the cost was estimated at £8,000.

Despite requesting rough cast walls, the City Architect was satisfied with red pressed brick to the lintels of the first-storey windows, and also the scheme of panelling and skylights on the upper section. Accordingly, on 13 April 1914 an interim warrant was issued, allowing construction to commence.

John McCartney was born in Glasgow in 1866. He had an impressive CV in respect of football clubs he had played for, beginning with Cartvale FC. He also played for Thistle FC, Rangers, Cowlairs, Newton Heath, Luton and Barnsley before becoming their secretary/manager in 1901. His career in management continued with St Mirren, whom he joined in 1904. McCartney's experience as a footballer stood him in good stead in management and he took the Paisley Buddies to the Scottish Cup final in 1908, only to lose to Celtic. But his managerial skills caught the eye of the directors of Hearts, who appointed him to the manager's post in 1910, replacing James McGhee. McCartney had an eye for a good player and very soon he put together a formidable side which would undoubtedly have won honours but for the intervention of the Great War. But it was during that time that John McCartney displayed more than managerial skills when he was deprived of his star players by the war. As a man he had many fine attributes and he needed them all as he strived to keep Hearts afloat during those dark times. McCartney didn't just work with one hand tied behind his back – sometimes it was with both. He received news of the deaths, wounds and missing-in-action reports of his players on active service with a brave face even although he was being torn apart inside. His display of restrained emotion was difficult. In October 1919 he left Edinburgh, and in 1920 was appointed manager of Portsmouth. Hearts acted quickly to find a successor for the departed McCartney and, remarkably, appointed his son Willie to the post at thirty years of age. There are varying stories as to his reasons for leaving; the loss of so many of his player during the war years did have an effect on the manager, but let us just remember him for what he was – a great. John McCartney, a man who will forever live in the folklore of Heart of Midlothian, returned to Edinburgh in later years and passed away in Scotland's capital city on 18 January 1933.

A gold medal presented to John McCartney by the Hearts Board of Directors in 1914 as a goodwill gesture for services rendered.

The reverse side of the medal.

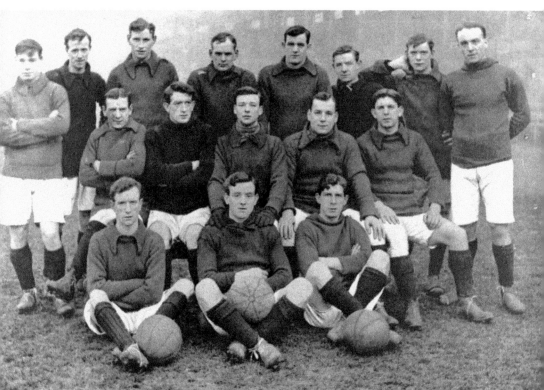

Opposite top: The Hearts party in Denmark in the close season of 1914. The team defeated a Copenhagen Select 2-1 and then also defeated a Danish international team by the same score two days later, with both Hearts' goals coming from Willie Wilson. From left to right, standing (players only): Archie Boyd, Harry Wattie, Tom Gracie, Willie Wilson. Seated: George Sinclair, Paddy Crossan, Peter Nellies, Duncan Currie, Bob Mercer. Front: Harry Graham and Alfie Briggs.

Opposite bottom: The Hearts squad for the 1913/14 season. From left to right, back row: Willie Wilson, Harry Wattie, Percy Dawson, Tom Allan, Robert Currie, George Currie, Paddy Crossan and David Taylor. Middle row: Alfie Briggs, Duncan Currie, Charles Hallwood, Louis Abrams, Willie Scott. Front row: Robert Malcolm, James Frew and Annan Ness.

Below: Heart of Midlothian's famous squad for the 1914/15 season. From left to right, back row: John Blackhall, Archie Boyd, Norman Findlay, James Speedie, Ernie Ellis. Middle row: Jimmy Duckworth, Robert McIntosh, James Frew, James Varty, Charles Hallwood, Annan Ness, Robert Malcolm, William Aitken, Elias Furst, Chairman,Walter Scott. Front row: Alfie Briggs, Harry Wattie, Tom Gracie, Peter Nellies, Willie Wilson, James Low, Bob Mercer. Seated on the ground: Paddy Crossan and Duncan Currie.

The impressive new Main Stand in 1914.

Above and opposite: Action shots from a Hearts *v*. Third Lanark League game played at Tynecastle on 25 October 1913 which finished 0-0. Note the old stand in the background, which was taken down to make way for the new stand designed by 'Engineering Archie'.

(1.) Crossan, if seen stopping a rush of Third players. (2.) Taylor, the other Simach back, proceeds to tackle Milne, the Third centre. (3.) Low and No, on the right, break away, leaving Riley sitting on the ground. ("Evening News" Photos.

Due to the demolition work, Hearts' chairman, Elias Furst, asked the president of Hibernian, John Farmer, for the use of Easter Road in order to complete the season's fixtures. This was generously given, free of charge, and on 18 April Hearts beat Raith Rovers 2-0 in a League match at their rivals' ground.

The principal contractors were Edinburgh companies Redpath Brown Ltd (steelwork, costing £3,298) and J. Duncan & Sons (brickwork and joinery, costing £4,249). Although Hearts had £4,000 in the bank, it was considered necessary to transfer Percy Dawson to Blackburn Rovers for a British record fee of £2,500. Dawson was paid £500 for his services and the balance of £2,000 was placed in the building fund. It has to be said that construction was not without serious problems, as major items, such as the cost of the decking on seat beams, dispersing passages and the front terraces, were missed on the building schedules. Dealing with these issues pushed up the total cost and caused a long delay in completion. In addition, it caused cash-flow problems for the contractors, which reflected badly on the club. However, when the stand was completed in October 1914 it was the most advanced in Scotland, running the whole length of the field, with 4,100 seats and 6,000 standing places under cover. There were excellent arrangements for the distribution and dispersal of crowds, modern toilet facilities, electric lighting, and extensive space for the players and the referee.

The Board of Directors decided that a formal opening would be inappropriate, although they did instruct a tablet to be placed on the outside wall, giving details of the directors involved in the construction project.

The Hearts support was looking forward to the opening of the 1914/15 season. Hearts' first game of the new season was scheduled to take place on 15 August, against none other than reigning champions Celtic. The Hearts fans couldn't wait and dreamt of their fine team collecting the honours in Scottish football in the coming season, and hopefully for years to come.

A nineteen-year-old by the name of Gavrilo Princip broke into their dream and turned it into a nightmare. On 28 June, in Sarajevo, this youth assassinated the heir to the Austro-Hungarian Empire, Archduke Franz Ferdinand, with a Browning automatic pistol and lit the fuse for a conflict on a global scale. A domino effect saw nations queuing to make war. On 1 August Germany declared war on Russia, and two days later on France. After weeks of mounting tension, it was clear that a major European war could not be avoided. The following day, the German Army swept into

Belgium. The invasion of Belgium brought Britain into the war. The British Government issued the obligatory ultimatum, demanding immediate cessation of hostilities and German withdrawal, which was ignored. On hearing the news that all the major powers in Europe were now at war, Sir Edward Grey, Britain's Foreign Secretary, remarked in a memorable phrase that: 'The lamps are going out all over Europe, we shall not see them lit again in our lifetime.' Suffice it to say that neither he, nor his European counterparts, nor the chiefs of staff, nor for that matter anyone else had the least idea of what the outbreak of the Great War implied for European civilization. It was a war that would cost millions of lives, see the map of Europe redrawn and social unrest and upheaval everywhere.

For his part, Gavrilo Princip was spared the death penalty by virtue of his age and was given a twenty-year jail sentence. He had been a member of a group of dissidents calling themselves the Young Bosnians, a secret society for students of peasant origins. In essence, they were terrorists. Princip was of slight build and stature, with a complete lack of personality, and he wanted to be noticed by people who had thought of him as a 'nobody'. After achieving notoriety by way of the murder, he explained himself by saying, 'Wherever I went, people took me for a weakling.'

Almost immediately, Hearts were deprived of the services of two of their playing staff. Neil Moreland and Scottish international George Sinclair, who were Army reservists, were called up. Because of the size of the playing staff at the club it was felt that this would not have an overly negative effect on the team.

From mining stock, Neil Moreland was a Broxburn lad, having been born to David and Susan Moreland at 160 Holygate Place, Broxburn, in July 1893. As a teenager he worked as a shale miner. He was signed by Hearts in February 1914 from the junior club Pumpherston Rangers as a backup for Percy Dawson, who was sold to Blackburn Rovers the following month. Moreland played three League games that season and two other competitive games in the North Eastern Cup, scoring two goals. Because of work the family later moved to the mining village of Tarbrax in Lanarkshire. Moreland was a member of the Territorial battalion, the 8th Highland Light Infantry. Rising to the rank of sergeant, he later served in the 7th Royal Scots on attachment from the HLI and was wounded in action on three separate occasions. He was first wounded at the Gallipoli Peninsula in July 1915, when fighting the Turks, when he sustained injuries to his left arm. Neil returned from active service and was re-signed by

Hearts in April 1916. He played two League games later that month and went home to Tarbrax to work in the shale mines. His last game for Hearts was a friendly in January 1919 against a Canadian XI and in April of that year he was released from Tynecastle after a total of seven competitive games and two goals. Neil Moreland's true potential was knocked out by the war but he joined Broxburn United and later signed for Albion Rovers and Lanarkshire side Dykehead.

He had two older brothers, William and David, who also served their country. William received wounds to his head in October 1915. His brother David, who also resided in Tarbrax, was killed in action at the Somme on 19 September 1917, leaving his wife to bring up a young child.

George Sinclair was a regular soldier who had left the Army in 1905 but was still classed as an Army reservist. He had been signed for Hearts by John McCartney in May 1908 from Second Division side Leith Athletic and was an exceptional winger and one of the club's all-time great players. However, his peak years were interrupted by the Great War and as a result George ended his career with a derisory three Scottish international caps. His dazzling wing play became a feature of the team and George was to earn many local medals during his career, but sadly none at national level. Sinclair supplied the ammunition for the strikers, but he was also a regular goalscorer with 48 goals in some 355 competitive games. He was a member of the Hearts squad that toured Scandinavia in 1912 and 1914, the club's first overseas tours. George also helped Hearts to the Scottish Cup semi-finals in 1912 and 1913 and added League international caps. In 1914 he received a Testimonial game against Everton and then as a reservist was immediately called up in August 1914 at the start of the Great War. He played no football for a year while serving as a driver in the Royal Field Artillery and took part in the first battle involving British troops at Mons in Belgium. George's tour of service ended in October 1915 and he returned to Edinburgh to work with the tramway company. He was immediately re-engaged by Heart of Midlothian and looked a class act among the guest and local junior players who kept the club going. George helped Hearts to reach the Victory Cup final in 1919 but the game was lost 3-0 to St Mirren and he never again came close to major honours. In April 1920 he received a second Testimonial game and 10,000 fans watched an East v. West game which ended 1-1. He assisted Hearts to reach the Scottish Cup semi-finals in 1921 and finish third in the League. Hearts released him on 30 April 1921 and he signed for Dunfermline Athletic. He later plied his trade with Cowdenbeath before running a very successful public house, Sinclair's Bar, at the top of Easter Road. In December 1959 George passed away in Edinburgh's Royal Infirmary at the age of seventy five.

Initially it was proposed that the start of the new football season be postponed, but despite misgivings in some quarters the fixtures went ahead as planned. The outbreak of war had occurred within ten days of the beginning of the new season and the easiest thing to do appeared to be to continue as normal. The Government was prepared to allow association football to continue on a modified scale, provided, eventually, that no one should make his entire living from playing the game. There was also a hidden agenda on the part of the powers that be. They saw the football grounds as excellent theatres for recruitment. Regular soldiers visited them on match days and made strenuous and successful efforts to persuade other spectators to 'take the shilling'.

On 15 August, the current League champions, Celtic, arrived in the west end of Edinburgh from the east end of Glasgow for the much-awaited opening game of the season.

Watched by a good attendance of 18,500 in glorious sunshine, Hearts' League campaign got off to a flier with a 2-0 victory over the Glasgow side, with the opening goal scored by Harry Wattie. It was a hard-earned win, with Bob Mercer being a virtual passenger in the second half due to sustaining an injury to his knee. As expected, the Celtic forward line applied immense pressure to the Hearts rearguard after going behind and 'keeper Archie Boyd was frequently called into action. With a few minutes remaining, the Hearts fans were in raptures when a new signing, centre forward Tom Gracie, rounded off a perfect day for the Tynecastle men when he scored the all important second goal. Champions Celtic couldn't come back from that hammer blow and there were ecstatic scenes when the referee's whistle brought the curtain down on a famous victory. The war was very quickly forgotten for a brief time as the Hearts support revelled in the defeat of the Glasgow giants.

Hearts followed up their opening day win with a 3-1 defeat of Raith Rovers at Stark's Park, Kirkcaldy. Never an easy venue to take full points from, Hearts produced a capital performance in the Fifers' backyard with a Willie Wilson first-half strike and a Harry Graham brace in the second half. But could the good form be maintained? The answer to that question was an emphatic 'yes' as the crowds began to flock to Tynecastle in great numbers. There were 16,000 inside the ground to see Third Lanark easily overcome by a vastly superior side by two goals to nil. Harry Graham gave Hearts the lead in the first half, with Robert Malcolm adding a second goal with ten minutes to go. But for the heroics of Third Lanark's Scotland international goalkeeper, Jimmy Brownlie, the score would have been more emphatic.

Then news filtered through of a defeat of a quite different nature. The British Expeditionary Force was being pushed back by the Germans from Mons and had suffered great losses to their manpower. At that time, regular Army personnel numbered less than 250,000 and it soon became obvious that recruitment was of the utmost importance. In Britain there was no compulsory military service – it was done on a voluntary basis. Suddenly, it was felt by some that conscription should be enforced in order to swell the numbers the armed services required, but support for this was still lukewarm.

In the middle of August, John McCartney decided to allow the authorities into Tynecastle on match days in an effort to encourage recruiting among the men on the terraces and in the stands. McCartney then arranged for all the playing staff to take part in weekly drill sessions in preparation for the possibility of military service. These drill sessions were to take place at Grindlay Street Hall. As the months rolled on and more news of the fighting and loss of life in Belgium and France reached home, the clamour for conscription increased.

Meanwhile, on the football front, Hearts' good form continued and among their most notable wins was a 2-1 defeat of Rangers at Ibrox on Saturday 19 September in front of an amazing attendance of 41,000. The importance of the game was not lost on McCartney. Rangers had dropped an unexpected point in a 1-1 draw with Dundee at Dens Park the previous week, leaving them a point behind Hearts, and a victory over McCartney's men would see them top of the League for the first time that season. McCartney's plan was for his players to play it 'tight' in the opening stages of the game as he knew that Rangers, urged on by their massive support, would go for an early opener.

McCartney fielded a strong Hearts team, with the following line-up: Boyd; Crossan, Currie; Briggs, Scott, Nellies; Low, Wattie, Gracie, Graham, Wilson.

Before Hearts had time to settle they found themselves a goal down. After only a minute's play, they were stunned when Willie Reid gave Rangers the lead after a goalmouth scramble.

In the words of Scotland's national bard, Robert Burns, 'The best laid plans o' mice and men gang aft a-gley [often go awry].'

Hearts hotly disputed the legality of the goal and the referee, Mr Murray of Stenhousemuir, consulted his linesman. After some deliberation the goal was allowed to stand. Thereafter the Hearts defence had to withstand a fair amount of pressure while, as predicted by McCartney, the huge Rangers contingent roared on their favourites. But the Hearts boys in defence stood shoulder to shoulder and gradually their forwards began to take a grip on the game. Their play was rewarded when Tom Gracie equalised with a goal that this time Rangers disputed. Herbert Lock, the Rangers 'keeper, held a shot from Willie Wilson but Gracie, following up strongly, bundled goalie and ball over the line.

In the fifty-ninth minute Hearts' joy was unrestrained when Harry Wattie gave them the lead after he connected with a cross by Wilson to put the ball past Herbert Lock. The goal proved to be the winner in a compelling game of football. What made the win even sweeter was that this was the Light Blues' first defeat of the season. Aye, life was pleasing down Gorgie way for the support as they enjoyed seeing their team occupy the lofty League position, and undefeated to boot.

Celtic, at this time, were well behind the leaders as the top half of the League showed.

	Played	Won	Lost	Drawn	For	Against	Points
HEARTS	6	6	0	0	16	2	12
AYR UNITED	6	4	1	1	10	4	9
RANGERS	6	4	1	1	10	5	9
AIRDRIEONIANS	6	3	1	2	7	4	8
CLYDE	5	3	1	1	5	2	7
ABERDEEN	6	3	2	1	9	6	7
GREENOCK MORTON	6	2	1	3	13	14	7
CELTIC	5	2	1	2	11	8	6

Two days later, on Monday afternoon, Hearts reinforced their intentions to win the championship by defeating second-placed Ayr United by a solitary goal, scored by James Low in the first half. It was a bruising encounter with the 'Honest Men' being quite physical in their play which, incidentally, did not lack ability. Hearts had to play the whole of the second half with Low a virtual passenger, due to being injured shortly after he had given his team the lead. It was a tremendous struggle between the two sides, which kept the 12,000 crowd on their toes right to the finish, with Tom Gracie and Harry Wattie coming close to increasing Hearts' slender lead in the final stages. It had been a hard, dour fight with the Ayrshire team but Hearts gave as good as they got, which must have pleased McCartney, who knew that the game had been the most physical demanding task his team had faced so far that season, and they had emerged with flying colours.

On 7 November, Hearts recorded a hard earned 2-1 win over Clyde at Celtic Park. The 'Bully Wee' were being temporarily accommodated at Celtic's ground for their home games. Hearts had gone behind when Black scored for Clyde after a mix-up in the Hearts defence but Tom Gracie brought the Maroons level. It was a ding-dong second half, with both sides giving everything, but with ten minutes remaining Gracie scored what proved to be the winner. After fourteen games played, the only dropped points had come in a surprise defeat at Dumbarton and a draw at Tynecastle against Queen's Park. The game against Dumbarton on 3 October was one that Hearts should not have lost. Even with a weakened side due to injuries, they twice led in the game before Dumbarton equalised with a penalty and then scored the winner near the end. The 2-2 draw against the 'Spiders' was a combination of poor finishing and overdoing fancy footwork, allowing Queen's Park, placed low in the League, to snatch a draw. Nonetheless, Heart of Midlothian sat proudly at the top of the Scottish League. But it was now Celtic, not Rangers, who posed a threat to Hearts' League championship aspirations as they began to put a good run of form together which saw them climb quietly up the League placings until they occupied pole position.

	Played	Won	Lost	Drawn	For	Against	Points
HEARTS	14	12	1	1	31	9	25
CELTIC	14	9	2	3	34	14	21
MORTON	13	6	1	6	30	21	18

NOVEMBER 1914

There was a cold, biting wind sweeping round Tynecastle on the afternoon of Saturday 14 November 1914 but the Hearts fans in the 12,500-strong crowd weren't affected by the weather that winter's day. They were being kept warm by their team's display in taking Falkirk apart in a League game. The Edinburgh side were 2-0 ahead through goals from Willie Wilson and Harry Wattie and were playing some outstanding football. At the interval, an appeal was made by the Queen's Own Cameron Highlanders for volunteers for the war effort but the appeal fell mainly on deaf ears. When the final whistle sounded, the victory kept Hearts at the top of the Scottish First Division and if the rich vein of form was to continue, they would undoubtedly be League champions come the end of the season. As the Hearts fans began to make their way along Gorgie Road in the gathering darkness to the warmth and comfort of their homes, they were in great spirits. After witnessing another tremendous display from their favourites, they had every right to be full of hope and confidence. All that was about to change very soon and life as they had known it would never be quite the same again.

Back at Tynecastle, there had been an unexpected development: James Speedie, the Hearts winger, had heeded the call to arms and joined up. McCartney was so moved by Speedie's decision that he sat down and penned a letter to James's mother and father, expressing his admiration for their son.

The *Edinburgh Evening Dispatch* proudly proclaimed 'Three Hearts men with the Colours now'. On Monday 16 November a letter was published in the *Edinburgh Evening News* that enraged those within the Hearts dressing room. Under the name of 'The Soldier's Daughter', it read: 'While Hearts continue to play football, enabled thus to pursue their peaceful play by the sacrifice of the lives of thousands of their countrymen, they might adopt, temporarily, a nom de plume, say "The White Feathers of Midlothian".'

On Friday 20 November, it was reported that Sir George McCrae had been granted permission by the Home Office to raise and command a battalion in the field with enlistment beginning almost immediately. The ball was rolling.

Shortly after that, John McCartney was asked by Sir James Leishman if he could meet with him at Leishman's shop premises in George Street. Sir James was the chairman of the National Health Insurance Commission for Scotland and was a close friend of Sir George McCrae. He followed the fortunes of Hearts and had provided unpaid consultancy work for the club over many years due to his business and financial expertise. It was there that McCartney learned from Sir James of the country's shortage of manpower to fight the war. It was a bleak picture that was painted. During the conversation, Sir George McCrae arrived unannounced. In later years McCartney would state that he didn't know if it was accident or design that had brought Sir George to Sir James'. McCrae immediately cut to the

R. MERCER
(HEARTS.)

Bob Mercer. Before the outbreak of the war, Bob Mercer, or 'Big Bob', was considered to be the finest centre half in Scotland and, but for his military service, which destroyed his football career and also his personal life, he would have made many more than his two full international appearances for Scotland and five representative games for the Scottish Football League.

Bob was born in the village of Avonbridge, Stirlingshire, on 21 September 1889 but his father, who came from the Borders, worked in the textile industry and the family frequently moved around the country, eventually settling in the town of Haddington. At football, Bob excelled at centre half, when this position involved both defending and moving forward to prime the attack. Standing at over 6 feet in height and weighing almost 13 stone, Bob's physical presence dominated the opposition forwards and in addition, his tactical brain and passing skills earned him the title 'Mastermind of Football'. Bob rose to the top with Gala Hailes Villa (a Border league side which disbanded in 1907) and Selkirk before signing for Second Division Leith Athletic in May 1908 at the age of nineteen. He was a star turn in the port and his talent didn't go unnoticed down Gorgie way and in June 1909 Hearts paid its local rivals the princely sum of £100 to secure Bob's services. With his all-round skill, the powerful youngster quickly became established in the first team. Indeed, in March

1912, Bob won his first full international cap and later that year he took part in Hearts' first overseas tour (to Scandinavia). This led to big-money offers from Aston Villa, Burnley and Manchester United that Hearts rejected.

In the 1914/15 season, he captained the team that looked like becoming Scottish champions, only to lose out to Celtic. Another huge factor in Hearts not winning the title that season was the loss of Mercer for much of the campaign, due to surgery on a torn knee ligament. This also prevented him from joining his colleagues in McCrae's Battalion. In addition to playing football, Bob worked with the tramway company during the early period of the war, but as his knee had not fully recovered and would not stand up to route marches, he joined the Royal Garrison Artillery (1st Lowland, City of Edinburgh) on 30 October 1916. His football was disrupted by Army training in the early months of 1917 and in January 1918 he left to serve on the Western Front. Bob was wounded and severely gassed at the Somme later that year. However, he fought back and regained a level of fitness that saw him return to the Hearts side which beat Clydebank 3-1 away from home on 8 February 1919. A week later, he made his long-awaited return to Tynecastle in a League game against Queen's Park. A massive cheer went up from the 12,000-strong crowd when Bob led the team onto the pitch. Another one of their 'sons' had come back.

In August 1919 Bob received a Testimonial match against a Glasgow XI which was appreciated because his health was bad, and indeed in December he contracted pneumonia and was seriously ill for months. Bob never fully recovered his best form and continued to suffer the effects of gas poisoning, often complaining of chest pains and breathing difficulties. After taking specialist advice, he was asked to consider retirement and he left Tynecastle in the summer of 1921. He made a brief comeback with Dunfermline Athletic in September 1921 and then eventually returned to Hearts in a coaching capacity in August 1925, looking after the Hearts youngsters. On Friday 23 April 1926 Bob took a young Hearts XI to play a friendly game against Selkirk at Ettrick Park. He had been specially invited to play at the ground where his senior career had commenced. Only a few minutes into the game, Bob collapsed to the ground unconscious. First aid was rendered and a doctor summoned but at 7.05 p.m. Bob Mercer was pronounced dead at the age of thirty-six. The match was immediately abandoned. Sadly, Bob Mercer was another belated victim of the Great War.

Above: The iconic photograph taken at Tynecastle on 25 November 1914 showing the players who enlisted that day. From left to right, back row: John McCartney, Ernie Ellis, Tom Gracie, Duncan Currie and Jimmy Duckworth. Middle row: Willie Wilson, Norman Findlay, Bob Preston and Harry Wattie. Front row: Alfie Briggs, Jimmy Frew and Annan Ness, holding Blackie the cat. Blackie, whose job was to 'take care' of mice within Tynecastle, had crept into the photo just as it was about to be taken. Jamie Low is missing from the line-up as he had to leave early to attend a class at Edinburgh University.

Below: This photograph of the men appeared in the *Edinburgh Evening News.* It shows an inset of James Low and Blackie is nowhere to be seen.

chase and asked McCartney about the possibility of some of the Hearts players joining the battalion being raised by him, telling him that such actions would make for a large following and a speedy formation of the unit. McCartney informed him that he alone could not make that decision – it would require a board meeting of the club's directors. On his return to the ground, McCartney assembled the club's directors and informed them of the meeting with McCrae and the proposals made. Initially, they were shocked at the prospect of them not having a team. The club was already in debt due to the construction of the new main stand at a cost which would escalate to over £12,000. They discussed the options open to them and realised that by losing the nucleus of the team, the League championship would be compromised and obviously the club's debt would increase. But despite all this, the directors decided unanimously to leave the final decision to the players. Following the board meeting, McCartney gathered his boys in the dressing room and, after sitting them down, told the players about the Board of Directors' decision. In a soft voice, he asked that the players who were willing to enlist should stand. The players had already discussed the matter among themselves with regards to enlisting. It is difficult to imagine the thoughts going through their minds at that time, especially the ones who were married. There were questions about how enlisting would affect their respective contracts with the club. If they did enlist, where would they be sent to serve? Would they serve together? They sat in silence – then a decision was made. Their contract was with their country, not their club. Almost to a man, they stood up.

That afternoon, after being medically examined and passed fit for service, eleven Heart of Midlothian players enlisted in Sir George McCrae's battalion: Alfred Briggs, Duncan Currie, Tom Gracie, Jamie Low, Harry Wattie, Willie Wilson, Ernie Ellis, Norman Findlay, Jimmy Frew, Annan Ness and Bob Preston. Five others were turned down because of medical reasons, the most notable being the captain, Bob Mercer, who was recovering from a serious injury to his knee. The others were George Bryden, diagnosed as having a weak heart; Harry Graham, who was asthmatic; Willie Aitken, who had developed tuberculosis; and Walter Scott, who had rheumatic fever. The War Office regulations were very strict and stated that no volunteer would be accepted if they had a history of respiratory illness.

Such was the determination of Walter Scott, or 'Wattie' as he was known, to enlist that he later joined a queue of volunteers who were waiting their turn at the recruiting office in Castle Street. To his dismay, the doctor carrying out the examinations was the same one who had already turned him down. Wattie was sent packing, cursing his luck as he went. Bob Mercer and Harry Graham, however, were conscripted in 1916.

Three players who didn't join up immediately were Paddy Crossan, Archie Boyd and his younger brother, Jimmy. The Boyd brothers wanted a bit more time to discuss the matter with their parents; Paddy just wanted a bit more time. There was an 'edge' to Crossan: he would go, of that there was no doubt, but in his own time. When the Boyd brothers' mother heard their intentions that evening when they returned to their house in Mossend, West Calder, she was shocked. Mrs Boyd declared that she would only allow one of her sons to join up as someone had to remain at home to support the family. The truth of the matter was that it would be bad enough losing one of her boys to the war; two would be unthinkable. Mrs Boyd, with tears in her eyes, left the two brothers alone in the room to make the decision as to which one of them would be left behind. The brothers looked at each other as they tried to come to terms with what their mother had said. Young Jimmy made the decision. Archie was engaged to be married and had more to lose. Mrs Boyd accepted Jimmy's unselfish act with a heavy heart, as did Archie. The scenario in the Boyd household must have been much the same in other homes when the other players had broken the news to their respective families. A lot of tears would have been shed in houses in and around the city of Edinburgh. Paddy and Jimmy put pen to paper two days later. The Heart of Midlothian football club had given Sir George two more of their family.

In the HMFC 'Report by Directors' to the Shareholders' AGM in July 1915, it was stated that 'the lead established by these gallant youths reverberated through the length of the land'.

Some 600 supporters and shareholders followed suit and joined up.

When the news of the enlistment became public, it captured the nation's imagination. The story was front page news in newspapers the length and breadth of the land, drawing forth eulogies from all quarters.

But there was still a League championship to be won and the following Saturday the League leaders travelled through to Lanarkshire to take on Hamilton Academical at Douglas Park. If the war was on the minds of the Hearts players, it didn't show as they chalked up a fine 3-1 victory, with goals from Willie Wilson, Tom Gracie and Harry Graham, with Harry Wattie being the main architect of the win.

The recruitment drive was now in full flow and then Hearts released a statement to the press which would send it into overdrive.

The Board of Directors of Heart of Midlothian Football Club hereby make a strong appeal to their supporters to join Sir George McCrae's Battalion. It is the earnest desire of the directors that an entire 'Hearts Company' be formed of players, ticket holders and general followers. The players have shown the way and it is now up to the other sections named to complete the requisite number. For the information of intending recruits, be it noted that the recruiting office is situated at 1 Castle Street. Heart of Midlothian applicants are requested to state when enlisting that they wish to be included in the Hearts Company.

Now then, young men, as you have followed the old club through adverse and pleasant times, through sunshine and rain, roll up in your hundreds for King and Country, for right and freedom. Don't let it be said that footballers are shirkers and cowards. As the club has borne an honoured name on the football field, let it go down in history that it also won its spurs on the field of battle.

Who could ignore the call to arms? The statement had the desired effect and very soon young men from all over, including footballers from seventy-five football clubs, junior and senior, among them Raith Rovers, Falkirk, Dunfermline and Hibernian, were flocking to Edinburgh to enlist.

The 75 clubs were: Armadale; Arniston Rangers; Bathgate; Bo'ness; Bonnyrigg Rose Athletic; Boroughmuir School; Broughton Higher Grade School; Broxburn Shamrock; Broxburn United; Civil Service Strollers; Colinton Wednesday; Cowdenbeath; Crossgates Thistle; Cupar Violet; Dalkeith Thistle; Dunfermline Athletic; Eastern; East Fife; Edinburgh Corinthians; Edinburgh & Leith Fish Trades; Edinburgh & Leith Postmen; Edinburgh Nomads; Edinburgh Renton; Edinburgh Union; Edinburgh University; Falkirk; Fisherrow Shop Assistants; Gala Fairydean; Heart of Midlothian; Hearts of Beath; Heriot-Watt Training College; Hibernian; Inverkeithing United; Kinleith Thistle; Kinleith Ramblers; Kirkcaldy United; Ladybank Violet; Leith; Leith Ivanhoe; Leith Police; Leith Provident; Leith Shop Assistants; Leith Wednesday; Leslie Hearts; Linlithgow Rose; Loanhead Mayflower; Moray House; Mossend Burnvale; Musselburgh Athletic; Musselburgh Juniors; Newtongrange Star; Niddrie Bluebell; Peebles Rovers; Penicuik Juniors; Pharmacy United; Portobello Thistle; Pumpherston Rangers; Raith Rovers; Rosewell Rosedale; St Bernard's; St Cuthbert's Athletic; St Leonard's United; Saughton Athletic; Shaftesbury Juveniles; Shandon Athletic; Tranent Juniors; Tynecastle Wednesday;

Valleyfield Athletic; Vale of Grange; Vale of Leithen; Wallyford Thistle; Warrender; Wemyss Athletic; West Calder Hearts; and West End Athletic. A brotherhood of sportsmen.

The first Edinburgh Derby of the season was scheduled for Saturday 5 December and prior to the game an invitation had been circulated to existing enlistees in the shape of a postcard from Sir George McCrae on the day before the game. It read:

> The Directors of the Heart of Midlothian Football Club have kindly offered free admission to the match at Tynecastle to-morrow 5th inst. to those who have enrolled in the new Service Battalion being raised by Sir George McCrae. Sir George McCrae will be glad if you will 'fall in' at the foot of Ardmillan Terrace at 1.45 pm.

Eight hundred men duly turned up and marched into the ground prior to kick-off. Both teams emerged to thunderous applause from the crowd. The weather was also thunderous and the game was played in appalling conditions as thunder, rain and sometimes hailstones swept across the west side of the city. Hearts then proceeded to sweep Hibernian back to Leith and their play lit up the grey leaden skies in a superb 3-1 win. Harry Wattie opened the scoring in the fifteenth minute after taking a pass from Jimmy Low. Hibs did well to keep the score at 1-0 but in the second half Hearts' pressure paid off when Harry Graham increased their lead. But then the Easter Road side found themselves back in the game, although somewhat fortuitously, when Jimmy Boyd, in attempting to clear a corner kick, put through an own goal. But the comeback was short-lived and Jimmy Low added a third to seal a great win.

Airdrieonians were next to be put to the sword at Tynecastle, through goals from Harry Wattie, Tom Gracie and Jimmy Low with Donaldson scoring the Lanarkshire side's solitary goal. It was a well-deserved victory as the game was played in difficult conditions, with sub-zero temperatures and sleet falling throughout.

On Boxing Day, Tom Gracie and Harry Wattie scored two apiece in a 4-0 win over Raith Rovers. The scoreline would have been greater but for a fine display by the Raith Rovers goalkeeper, Neish.

Before the end of the year a meeting was held by the Scottish League to discuss the general financial position within the game. It was unanimously agreed, with a view to assisting all clubs to complete their fixtures, to recommend all Second Division clubs to reduce their players' wages by not less than 50 per cent. This had the effect of flushing out not a few players into heavy industry. As a further cost-cutting measure, it was decided that the services of neutral linesmen would be dispensed with for the duration of the war. Less logically, given the decision to continue League football, it was felt that the running of the Scottish Cup competition would be inappropriate and the tournament was suspended.

The maximum wage for First Division players was reduced to £4 10s 0d per week and close-season wages became a thing of the past. Players would not now be paid between 1 May and the resumption of training in late July. Even this reduction proved wildly unrealistic and when it was decided to carry on the First Division the following season, it was claimed to be impossible to pay more than £1 per week. The First Division clubs indicated that they would continue to function in the 1915/16 season. The lower-division clubs had been losing money hand over fist and could not possibly contemplate another such season. They asked for the creation of two Scottish sectional leagues, East and West, but the First Division clubs refused to accede to this suggestion. The Second Division thereafter ceased to exist for the duration of the war.

On New Year's Day 1915, Hearts were not on League business; instead, they played Hibs at Easter Road in the final of the Wilson Cup. The silverware was duly won in a 2-1 victory. But it was the result of the Old Firm game taking place at Ibrox on 1 January that had the Hearts fans cheering. Rangers had overcome their bitter rivals 2-1 to still keep Hearts four points clear of Celtic, but with the added advantage of having a game in hand.

The following day, Hearts resumed League business with a visit to Brockville. Never the easiest of grounds to visit for Hearts, who had still to record a League win there, this game proved no exception. The weather in the days before the match had been a mixture of rain followed by severe frost, a thaw and then more rain. The playing surface, which was inches deep in mud where pools of water weren't lying, was certainly not conducive to good football. However, the farcical conditions, which knocked all science out of the game, resulted in a match that was exciting as a spectacle as both sides simply got on with it. Falkirk took the lead just before half-time through Ramsay. During the interval, the ground staff had to re-line areas of the pitch before the second half got underway. Shortly after resumption, Tom Gracie scored the all-important equaliser. There was no further scoring in what can be best described as a gruelling contest on a stamina-sapping pitch. In the interim, Celtic kept up the pressure on Hearts by beating Clyde 2-0 at Shawfield. The festive period games were completed on 4 January when Hamilton Academical 'first footed' Hearts. In a game played on a heavy surface, it was the Lanarkshire men who were the better side in the first half and Archie Boyd in the Hearts goal was by far the busier 'keeper. It was thanks mainly to him that the score remained 0-0 at the break. Strong words must have been spoken in the home side's dressing room at half-time as Hearts began the second half in whirlwind fashion. Two quick goals by Willie Wilson put paid to any hopes of the 'Accies' creating an upset and returning to Hamilton with all the points. In the end, Hearts were easy winners and just before the final whistle Tom Gracie added a third. Over in Glasgow, Celtic kept up their challenge with a 2-0 win over Kilmarnock.

By this time, the players' military training had begun and some of it consisted of going on long, exhausting runs in Edinburgh's Pentland Hills. It was not uncommon for them to arrive back in the late evening, sometimes as late as 10 p.m., and be back up at 6 a.m. for more drill and physical training. The Pentland Hills, as they are to this day, could be a dark, cold, wet, unwelcoming and formidable place, not just in the winter months but also in the summer. As a consequence some of the players suffered bouts of influenza from being exposed to the elements. Blisters on their feet also became a problem and although military training was necessary, it was not ideal preparation for vital games of football on a Saturday as Hearts chased their dream of winning the League. A case in point was the home game against Morton at Tynecastle on 9 January. The team struggled to find any fluency in their play and looked tired and jaded, even from the early stages of the game. Some of the players had even worn new boots, a size bigger than normal to allow extra room for the dressings on their blisters. A goal from Tom Gracie after fifteen minutes was all that separated the sides at the end of the ninety minutes in what was a below-par performance. It was at that juncture that some members of the press began to muse on whether the military training was having an adverse effect on the team. One man who was firmly of that view was the Hearts trainer, Jimmy Duckworth. He announced that in future he would accompany the players on their 'runs in the country' and be on hand to treat even the most minor of injuries as and when they happened. 'Duckie', as he was known to those in and around Tynecastle, was a character in his own right and was greatly respected by the management and playing staff.

Duckworth was a sixty-three-year-old bachelor who had no children of his own, but the Hearts lads were his family and Tynecastle was his home. Born in Gorton, Lancashire, as a young man he had become a successful runner over one mile and longer distances. When Jimmy stopped participating, he established his reputation as an accomplished trainer of professional runners. He then came north of the border to become trainer with Leith Athletic and in 1908 he was appointed in the same capacity at Hearts. Interestingly, when Jimmy Duckworth was interviewed for the position of trainer, another interviewee was none other than Bill Struth. Edinburgh born, Struth was employed as a trainer with Clyde at that time and had resided just round the corner from Tynecastle before moving to Glasgow. While living at Wheatfield Street, Bill Struth had assisted at Hearts, unpaid, with the team's training. Struth was also a Hearts shareholder and the shares register from 1905 showed his address to be 8 Wheatfield Street, Edinburgh, but in later years this was changed to 7 Edmiston Terrace, Copland Road, Glasgow. One must wonder how events would have turned out if Struth, who went on to become the most successful manager in the history of Rangers, had been selected for the post ahead of Duckworth.

'Duckie' often assisted the Scotland and Scottish League teams and also found time to train professional runners, one of whom was the celebrated Albert Downer. Duckworth trained the winner of the Powderhall Sprint, 1912. Jimmy Duckworth clearly knew his business and was commended by the Board of Directors for the fitness of the players. His views were often sought on team selections and player assessment. Jimmy made a speech to the players on the day of their enlistment, telling them that they were the sons he never had and that he was so proud of them. Back then trainers had a very important role in fitness, coaching, discipline and player assessment and Jimmy Duckworth was ably supported by his assistant trainer, Alex Lyon. Alex lived not far from Tynecastle, at 21 Westfield Road, with his wife Margaret and two young children. Like Jimmy Duckworth, he was particularly conscientious. Both these men played a crucial role in keeping the club operating during the early period of the war. They assisted the players with the physical problems caused by the military exercises and sometimes having to play a vital football match shortly after having returned from such a sojourn. Jimmy and Alex then began to go on these strength-sapping manoeuvres with the players throughout January and the players appreciated their presence, but tragedy was waiting just round the corner for the Lyon family.

In early 1915 the Government were introducing changes to everyday life and they launched an appeal for women to volunteer for war work. As more men enlisted, opportunities became available to break through barriers in industries which had up to that time been male dominated. This didn't just apply to munitions factories but to everyday employment such as driving taxis and trams. In Edinburgh, the latest addition to the ranks of working women included coal-carters. Females were now employed in bagging and delivering coal to households throughout Scotland's capital. By coincidence, the patriotic song 'Keep the Home Fires Burning ('Till the Boys Come Home)' was popular at that time, not just in Scotland and the rest of the country but in the trenches abroad, where the soldiers sang it while they thought of home and their loved ones waiting for them.

The annual rugby international between Scotland and England along with golf's British Open were suspended for the foreseeable future. In horse racing, the thoroughbred Templedowney won the last Scottish Grand National at Bogside in Ayrshire before racing suffered the same fate.

The Government, ever alert to the possible presence of enemy spies, decreed that photographs were now to be attached to the holders of British passports. The Scottish author John Buchan had his novel *The Thirty-Nine Steps* published by William Blackwood & Sons, Edinburgh. The plot focused on German spies operating in Britain and the central character of Richard Hannay caught not only the public's imagination but also that of the men serving afield.

On Saturday 16 January Dundee were the visitors to Tynecastle, while second-placed Celtic were at Brockville to take on Falkirk. It was a patched-up Hearts side who took to the field, with Harry Wattie missing from the line-up due to an ankle injury sustained in a fall the previous night and James Low also out due to a high temperature as the influenza blight took hold. Duncan Currie was also feeling unwell but played despite the misgivings of John McCartney. As one would expect, it was a poor performance from Hearts in the early stages of the game and fifteen minutes into the second half they were staring defeat in the face as the Dens Parkers led 2-0. But somehow they dug deep into their powers of resilience and in a fantastic five-minute spell they turned the game on its head. In the seventieth minute Tom Gracie pulled a goal back and three minutes later George Bryden levelled the scores. The cheers had hardly died down when Tom Gracie, from a free kick, scored what proved to be the winning goal.

At Brockville, Celtic kept up the pressure on the Gorgie men as they beat the 'Bairns' by virtue of a highly controversial second-half goal scored by

Andy McAtee. The Falkirk goalkeeper, Stewart, had actually held McAtee's shot but the referee adjudged that Stewart had carried the ball over the line and awarded the goal. It had now become a two-horse race for the League title, with the Edinburgh side still holding a three-point lead over the 'Hoops'. It was nail-biting stuff.

The top of the League was as follows:

	Played	Won	Lost	Drawn	For	Against	Points
HEARTS	25	22	1	2	60	15	46
CELTIC	26	20	3	3	63	20	43

But John McCartney was becoming increasingly concerned with regards to the physical condition of his playing staff and spoke of this after the game. On Thursday, following the game against Dundee, the players in McCrae's Battalion were inoculated and as a result some of them suffered severe reactions. Saturday saw the team travel to Glasgow to play Third Lanark while Celtic's game was cancelled due to freezing fog which had been hanging around since Friday night. At the end of the game, John McCartney ruefully reflected that perhaps it would have been better if the game against Thirds had suffered the same fate as Celtic's as his under-par side threw away a vital point on a frost-bound pitch. A postponement would have given his lads a well-earned rest. At Cathkin, in front of Third Lanark's biggest crowd of the season, Hearts led 1-0 at half time after Harry Graham had scored in the fifteenth minute. Harry Wattie added a second not long after the resumption and it looked as if the points were safe. Third Lanark, however, had an unbeaten home run to defend and set about Hearts, eventually scoring through Hannah. The Maroons were now hanging on grimly to their lead as fatigue began to set in – and then disaster. A long, dipping, speculative shot from Third Lanark's inside forward Walker seemed to deceive Archie Boyd in the Hearts goal and the ball ended up in the net. One would have expected the heads to go down but astonishingly Hearts recovered and found the guts and sheer determination to drive forward again and again, with the Third Lanark goal surviving many escapes in the dying minutes of the contest. The manager knew that his men were giving their all and couldn't in any way criticise them or ask for any more. Little did people know that some of his players had been on a military exercise the night before the game and had returned to their homes in the early hours of Saturday morning. Little or no sleep was not the ideal preparation for an important League game, one would have to say. Then came the toughest of all challenges so far in the League campaign – a visit to the east end of Glasgow, where Celtic lay in wait. But these Hearts had no fear. Their courage was epitomised by Tom Gracie, who struggled from his sick bed, where he had lain all week, to lead the line at Celtic Park. The fullness of Tom's illness would only come to light in the coming months. The Edinburgh side silenced the massive Celtic support in the crowd of over 50,000 when they took the lead through Harry Graham after only five minutes. But Celtic equalised through Andy McAtee, again under questionable circumstances. Many thought that he had used a hand to control the ball before putting it into the net, but the goal stood. There was no further scoring and the game finished with honours even. It had been a backs-to-the-wall display by Hearts but it was a far better point for them than it was for Celtic. The result meant that they still maintained their four-point lead over Celtic, with each having played twenty-seven games and now only eleven to go. This is how the top of the League table looked:

	Played	Won	Lost	Drawn	For	Against	Points
HEARTS	27	22	1	4	63	18	48
CELTIC	27	20	3	4	64	21	44

Kilmarnock were next up at Tynecastle on 6 February and despite having only three fully fit players, McCartney's men still managed to record a hard but well-earned 3-1 victory over the Ayrshire men. Willie Wilson put Hearts in front after twelve minutes and before half-time Tom Gracie had doubled their lead. In the second period of play, Kilmarnock came back strongly and Neil reduced the deficit with a well-taken goal. However, Harry Graham put the issue beyond doubt with a third goal. But the manager knew that his brave boys were almost running on empty, with the rigours of military training having an adverse effect, and mulled over whether or not they would make it over the finishing line. Meanwhile, in the west, Celtic still maintained their relentless pursuit of Hearts with a 2-1 win over St Mirren at Celtic Park.

Then came news that assistant trainer Alex Lyon had contracted bronchial pneumonia and had been admitted to Edinburgh Royal Infirmary. The night-time runs through the Pentland Hills in the sometimes Arctic conditions had proved too much for him.

A visit to Fir Park, Motherwell, was the next port of call. Paddy Crossan, who had spent all week in bed suffering from 'flu, returned to the fray for this vital fixture. He turned in a sublime performance in the 1-0 win. Harry Wattie scored the vital goal deep into the second half with a header from an Alfie Briggs free kick. In a game that was played in weather conditions that were cold and raw, a typical Lanarkshire winter, Motherwell had to play all of the second period with ten men after their inside forward Bond had the misfortune to break a leg. Celtic were down at Tail o' the Bank that day in what many thought would be an awkward fixture for them. As it transpired, they chalked up an easy 2-0 win over Greenock Morton, the goals coming in each half. The pressure was intense and then a tragic event happened that put everything into perspective.

On 14 February 1915, every single person connected to the Heart of Midlothian was stunned when they learned that Alex Lyon had passed away. He was thirty years of age. The club paid for Alex's funeral expenses and agreed to pay his widow the sum of £1 per week until the end of April 1915. His funeral took place at Dalry Cemetery, a short distance from his beloved Tynecastle, on 17 February. Alfie Briggs and Duncan Currie helped carry the coffin. Jimmy Duckworth, himself evidently unwell and against the wishes of his doctor, attended the funeral service to see his colleague and friend laid to rest and also assisted in carrying the coffin. The war had claimed its first victim from the Hearts family. Hearts made a further gesture by fielding an A team against an East of Scotland Junior Select at Tynecastle on 17 April 1915. The benefit match for Alex Lyon raised the sum of £59, which was sent to his widow Margaret, who greatly appreciated the kind and thoughtful gesture.

Hearts' following game was against Rangers at home but two days before the fixture some of the players received their second inoculation, this time for typhoid, and once again some suffered the effects. A big crowd was inside Tynecastle for the visit of the Light Blues and very quickly it was the Hearts support among the 23,500 who had the blues as the Ibrox men raced in to a two-goal lead, despite facing a strong wind, with goals from Willie Reid and Tommy Cairns. If that wasn't bad enough, Willie Wilson then missed a penalty for the Gorgie men. Hearts were dealt a further blow when at half-time Paddy Crossan, Alfie Briggs, Duncan Currie and Harry Wattie, clearly suffering from the effects of their recent inoculations, were violently sick. Two goals down and with four of his key players unwell, John McCartney must have felt as if his world was crashing all around him. But all four returned to the field of play, which inevitably inspired their teammates, and Hearts began to stamp their authority on the game. But the Rangers rearguard couldn't be breached and in a rare second-half attack, Reid scored a third goal in the sixty-fifth minute. The same player completed his hat-trick ten minutes later and it looked all over bar the shouting. With eight minutes remaining, Tom Gracie reduced the deficit with a well-taken penalty. It looked very much like a consolation goal but then four minutes later Jimmy Low scored Hearts' second goal with a tremendous drive. Suddenly the Glasgow giants began to look uncomfortable and two minutes later they were absolutely squirming as Willie Wilson scored a third with a swerving shot. By this time Tynecastle was alight as the Hearts support roared on their favourites as they continued to take the game to Rangers. Where this brave side were getting their reserves of strength and power from was anybody's guess as they fought for and contested every ball, driving Rangers further and further back. The tension was unbearable; and then in the final minute Willie Wilson struck a fierce drive which had the Rangers 'keeper Herbert Lock beaten all ends up. The Hearts fans' roars of 'goal' were quickly stifled as the ball rebounded from the post and back into play. When the final whistle was blown soon after, it sounded like music to the Rangers' players ears. The Hearts eleven trooped silently back to the dressing room; they had given their all but it wasn't enough. Word then came through that Celtic had scraped a 1-0 win over Dumbarton at Celtic Park. Eight games remaining and that four-point cushion had now been whittled down to two.

By this time it had all become too much for Jimmy Duckworth and he suffered a nervous breakdown. He was admitted to Edinburgh Royal Infirmary for complete rest. Tom Murphy, the groundsman, had been appointed assistant trainer by this time, replacing Alex Lyon, and he took over Jimmy Duckworth's duties in the interim. Murphy was a competent person and his temporary appointment met with 'Duckie's' approval. Murphy had also been a professional runner and a trainer of athletes and was held in high esteem by the manager and directors. After a few weeks' recuperation, Jimmy Duckworth was back at Tynecastle carrying out his duties, somewhat against the wishes of his doctor. The doctor was proved correct and Jimmy was readmitted to the Royal Infirmary but three weeks later he was once again at work for the club he loved. That was Jimmy – Hearts were simply his life. The man clearly loved Hearts unconditionally.

The next week Hearts made the short trip across the city to Easter Road while Celtic travelled across their city to Firhill to play Partick Thistle. In a fiercely contested game, Hibernian began with the perfect start when the unfortunate Paddy Crossan headed into his own net. Hearts simply rolled up their sleeves and Harry Graham equalised. Into the second half and that man Tom Gracie, so often the scorer of important goals, put Hearts ahead. The Tynecastle men could have been further in front but as so often in Derby games, the unexpected always happens. From a corner on the right, Hibernian's Robertson scored a dramatic equaliser. It was an exhausted Hearts side that returned to Gorgie that evening after the 2-2 draw. The newspaper *The Sunday Post* reported that the Hearts players looked a yard slower than their opponents and put it down the military training. It was a buoyant Celtic side that returned to Parkhead with full points, having beaten the 'Jags' 2-0. A single point now separated them.

The top of the League table was as follows:

	Played	Won	Lost	Drawn	For	Against	Points
HEARTS	31	24	2	5	72	25	53
CELTIC	31	24	3	4	71	22	52

Hearts got back on the winning trail with a 4-1 win over Dumbarton, courtesy of a Tom Gracie hat-trick and a single from Harry Graham. It was a tremendous display by Hearts and they played some great football throughout and maybe they were just going to make it over the finishing line after all. Celtic hammered Hibs 5-1 in Glasgow, their first goal coming via the penalty spot and the second by virtue of an own goal.

Airdrieonians' Broomfield was next up, giving Hearts the chance of extending their lead to three points as Celtic's game had been cancelled. They extended their lead, but only by two points after another 2-2 draw. In front of 12,000 spectators Hearts were two goals up after just fifteen minutes, Harry Graham scoring twice, but before the interval Airdrie's Jimmy Reid had reduced the leeway. The nerves were being shredded. Play in the second half was even and it looked as if Hearts were going to return home with maximum points. With fifteen minutes remaining, Jimmy Reid again broke through the Hearts rearguard to score for the 'Waysiders' and break the hearts of the Maroon faithful.

The top of League table was as follows:

	Played	Won	Lost	Drawn	For	Against	Points
HEARTS	33	25	2	6	78	28	56
CELTIC	32	25	3	4	76	23	54

It was then the turn of Partick Thistle to come to Tynecastle and they returned to Maryhill empty-handed as Hearts took all the points with a 3-1 win. Harry Wattie, Jimmy Low and Harry Graham were the men on the score sheet for Hearts, who were without the services of Nellies and Wilson. Again, Celtic didn't play that day as the inter-League game between Scotland and England was being held at Celtic Park. Peter Nellies and Willie Wilson were in the Scotland side, which was soundly beaten 4-1. Although Hearts had re-established the four-point lead, the Glasgow side had those two important games in hand. The champions did, however, play the following week, when they overcame Raith Rovers 3-1 at home. Meanwhile, Clyde were going down 2-0 at Tynecastle thanks to late goals from Jimmy Low and Tom Gracie. At one point the game looked to be heading for a 0-0 draw after Hearts had scorned numerous chances to go in front. But Hearts' win came at a cost, as Tom Gracie was admitted to the Royal Infirmary for tests and observations when he fell ill after the game. There wasn't much left in the locker as the illness surrounding the club really took hold. McCartney's boys were quite literally out on their feet but still they kept going.

The long trip north to the Granite City of Aberdeen beckoned for Hearts, with Tom Gracie and Willie Wilson missing from the team. Although Wattie played, it was obvious to everyone that he was unfit due to being ill. The train journey back to Edinburgh seemed to last much longer than normal after having dropped another point as the result of the 0-0 draw. This was Gracie's first absence from a League game since coming to Tynecastle. HMFC Board Room Minutes from 6 April 1915 gave the reason for his absence as suffering from the effects of inoculations. It was a noteworthy coincidence that this was the first time that season that Hearts had failed to score in a League game, although they did have chances to score at Pittodrie in front of a crowd in the region of 7,000. Robert Malcolm had replaced Gracie at centre forward but he got very little change out of the big, burly and dominant figure of Jock Wylie, the Dons' centre half.

Celtic didn't have a problem in the scoring stakes as they put three past Airdrieonians without reply at Celtic Park. Two days later, they defeated Queen's Park by the same margin at Hampden Park. With a game in hand, they were now only one point behind.

Another lengthy journey faced Hearts in the following away game as they visited Cappielow to play Greenock Morton. Amazingly, the night before the game, the Army had the enlisted players out on manoeuvres, arriving back just in time for them to get a few hours' sleep before catching the train to Greenock. At that juncture you would have thought that someone in the higher echelons of command in the British Army had a wager on Celtic retaining the League championship. You couldn't make it up. If that scenario had occurred in this day and age, the 'conspiracy theorists' would be having a field day. The telephone lines would be going into meltdown as they tried to contact the various radio stations' phone-ins. And they would have a strong case.

In the game at Greenock, Hearts missed two penalties. Gracie and Nellies were the sinners. Peter Nellies put his effort past the post and Tom Gracie sent his shot straight into the arms of the Morton goalie. Morton took full advantage of these costly misses and put two into the visitors' net either side of half time, the second coming from a penalty, with no reply from the visitors. Celtic also took full advantage by defeating Aberdeen 1-0 at home, their goal coming from Jimmy McMenemy in the first half, enabling them to go top of the League. Aberdeen had chances to take the lead but poor finshing let them down. In the second half it was one-way traffic as Celtic dominated and for long periods Aberdeen were hemmed in but the score remained the same. It has to be said that Celtic were the most consistent side in the country and a very strong and resilient outfit.

No words could possibly describe the feelings and thoughts of the Hearts party as they returned to Edinburgh that Saturday night. They knew that their chances of taking the title were extremely slim and it would require a major miracle to do so.

The League positions were as follows:

	Played	Won	Lost	Drawn	For	Against	Points
CELTIC	36	29	3	4	86	24	62
HEARTS	37	27	3	7	83	31	61

Consequently, it was a lacklustre Hearts team who went down 1-0 to St Mirren at Love Street the following Saturday, 17 April. The players came off the pitch at Love Street totally and utterly disconsolate, mentally and physically exhausted. They sat within the dressing room in numb silence, which was only broken by John McCartney entering the room. He looked round at the sweat- and tear-stained faces of these young men who had given him everything he could possibly have asked for as a manager. They had fought against all the odds to secure the League championship, which had become a bridge too far. When he eventually spoke, it was with a quiet but proud voice. McCartney simply said that nobody could have asked any more of them and that they had done themselves, the club and the support proud. With those few but very meaningful words, he left the room. McCartney had tears in his eyes as he stood alone in the changing room corridor within the main stand at Love Street. He knew within his heart that some of the players in the dressing room he had just left, who were due to go to France soon, would never play together again in a maroon jersey. McCartney was also burdened with the knowledge that one of his prominent players had been continuing to play for him despite having been diagnosed with an illness. The player in question had told no one other than his close family and his manager and wished that the matter remained confidential.

Celtic took the championship by virtue of a 4-0 win over Third Lanark.

The following is how the race for the League championship was described by the *Edinburgh Evening News*.

Saturday saw an end to the struggle between the Heart of Midlothian and the Celtic for the Scottish League Championship. The former lost at Paisley and the Celtic won at Cathkin and stand 3 points ahead with a game still to play. The Hearts have completed their programme. The Parkhead team are to be congratulated on retaining possession of the flag, but much sympathy will go out to Hearts, who put up a great fight, and at one time seemed almost certain champions. What effect military training may have on the form of the footballers is a matter for argument, but the fact remains that it was only after the majority of the Tynecastle players had enlisted that a deterioration of play set in.

Celtic drew their remaining game with Motherwell to win the title by four points.

There was no doubt that some people perceived that an injustice had been done but it was left to the newspapers to express the opinions held by many in the Scottish game. The *Evening News* stated:

Hearts have laboured these past weeks under a dreadful handicap, the likes of which our friends in the west cannot imagine. Between them the two leading Glasgow clubs have sent not a single prominent player to the Army. There is only one football champion in Scotland and its colours are maroon and khaki.

In an interview with the *Edinburgh Evening News*, John McCartney made a very moving statement to the newspaper. He said: 'They played at times so tired and sore that they could hardly stand yet they took Celtic to the last day of the season and left Rangers floundering 11 points behind. They gave their best throughout and that is all that anyone could ask. Edinburgh is proud of them.'

There is always something so sad, so forlorn about a team that takes second place: sympathy but no glory. But on this occasion Hearts had taken the glory. They didn't win the League championship but instead they had won something far more precious: they had won the hearts and admiration of the nation.

In the season's closing weeks it was obvious that the military training the Hearts players had to endure was a major factor in the Maroons not winning the Scottish League championship while not belittling Celtic's form in the run-in, which had been the model of consistency. But who knows what the outcome of the League might have been if the nation had remained at peace? Who knows what might have been in the years that lay ahead if the cream of Scottish football had not been destroyed in a war that not everyone wanted? Two questions that will forever remain unanswered.

Little did the 'Gorgie Faithful' realise away back then that it would take another forty-three years before the League flag would fly proudly over Tynecastle, when it was won with a record number of points in 1958, and that the journey that lay ahead of them would be a long, difficult and arduous one, with countless tears falling along the way. A journey that few other clubs in the country would have to endure. A journey that some would not return from. A journey that would never be forgotten but one that would be inspirational.

On 7 May 1915 the horror of the war continued when the Cunard liner *Lusitania* was sunk off the coast of Ireland after being torpedoed by a German U-boat. Around 1,200 people, including 124 Americans, lost their lives and the act brought condemnation from the President of the United States. Germany's response was that any ship found in the seas around Britain was fair game for attack.

On 22 May 1915, the country was again hit with the tragic news that a large number of soldiers had been killed. But this time the calamitous information that was received did not come from France or Belgium – it was from Scotland.

A multiple-train crash on the Glasgow–London line claimed the lives of 226 people, which included 214 Scottish soldiers, along with 246 casualties although the exact numbers were never established and tend to vary to this day.

The accident took place just before 7 a.m. when a crowded troop train travelling from Larbert to Liverpool was involved in a collision at Quintinshill, near Gretna. The troop train, which was one of five involved in a series of collisions, was transporting a battalion from the 1/7th Royal Scots, who were bound for Gallipoli. The resultant fires from the steam engines, coupled with gas leakages from the gas-powered lighting system on the troop train and the ammunition it was carrying, caused massive explosions as the fires quickly spread. Such was the magnitude of the inferno that it took the fire brigade until the next day to finally extinguish the flames and bring the situation under control.

It was later deemed that the accident was due to negligence on the part of the signalmen, George Meakin and James Tinsley, and they were both later found guilty of involuntary manslaughter and jailed. The majority of the dead were buried in Rosebank Cemetery, Edinburgh. The soldiers who were killed were mostly from Leith.

Quintinshill remains Britain's worst ever rail disaster. By a strange twist of fate, and some 14 miles to the north, seventy-three years after the train transporting the soldiers south had passed through the peaceful town of Lockerbie, 270 people lost their lives there in Britain's worst ever air disaster when Pan Am's *Maid of the Seas* was blown from the skies above the town.

After this tragedy the early months of summer passed swiftly by and then, all too soon, it was time to go for the Hearts lads in McCrae's Battalion – orders had come through for mobilisation. On the morning of 18 June, 1,100 soldiers marched proudly down the Mound and Market Street to Waverley Station to the sound of the pipes and drums. Thousands turned out to wish them a fond farewell and a safe return. The majestic and famous old Princes Street became gridlocked due to the huge numbers of well-wishers who had gathered there. Edinburgh Castle looked down proudly on the scene below. You could almost see the weather-beaten fortress nodding in approval.

Many years later, Craig Herbertson would write and perform 'Hearts of Glory' and the lyrics of his stirring but sad song describe the moment perfectly.

> This is my story
> This is my song
> It's a long way from Gorgie
> To the fields of the Somme
> Where they played tunes of glory
> As we marched along
> The pals o' the Sporting Battalion.
>
> From the Heart of Midlothian
> To the Waverley train
> The crowds they were singing
> An auld Scots refrain
> Our sweethearts and darlings
> Our bonnie wee bairns
> Were waving our flags
> And calling our names
>
> Sing Hearts of Glory
> Dawn and sunset
> Hearts of glory
> Lest we forget
> Young Scottish soldiers
> And soldiers unknown
> Who gave hearts of glory

On the southbound platform, emotional goodbyes and embraces were exchanged as they started to board. The train then began to move off. Slowly at first, then gathering speed, leaving behind the families, loved ones and the people who were tasked to look after the fortunes and the safe-keeping of the Heart of Midlothian while they were gone. By this time, enough had been learned about the horrors of the war for those remaining on the platform to realise that they may never see their husbands, sons, brothers, fathers and loved ones again. Some would return to Tynecastle to pull on the famous maroon jersey and run onto the field to the roar of the crowd. Some would return but, because of their wounds, injuries and mental scars, would be unable to play the beautiful game ever again; some wouldn't return at all.

John McCartney cut a lone figure, standing there on the platform watching his boys depart, never knowing when they would return or who would return. He later recalled: 'There was a moment, a long moment, of unexpected silence – of disbelief, I think, that it had come to this. I could not move. I stood quite still with my hand on Rawson's shoulder, and then I heard the cheering start again. The finest men I had ever known had gone.'

McCartney was devastated, but such was the mark of the man that later on in the day he held a meeting at Tynecastle with the remaining playing staff. McCartney's voice carried the resonance of certainty. He told them that in the coming season a great deal of pressure would be brought to bear, not just on the players but on everyone at the club, and that the task that lay ahead would be daunting in more ways than one. How prophetic those words uttered by the manager turned out to be. McCartney finished by saying, 'Do your best lads – that is all anyone could ask of you.'

The following is an extract from the HMFC Directors' Report to the Shareholders' AGM on 6 July 1915:

The advent of the Great European War has been responsible for many things. Concerning ourselves it is practically safe to assume that but for this world tragedy the Club would have finished in the position it held at the top of the League table for 35 out of 37 constituting the season. Financially the year would also have been a record one.

These considerations apart, a far higher and nobler record was established when, at the call of patriotism, sixteen of the players enlisted for active service. The lead established by these gallant youths reverberated throughout the length and breadth of the land, drawing forth eulogiums from all quarters.

Including George Sinclair and Neil Moreland, the former a Reservist and the latter a Territorial, who were both called up at the outbreak of the war, the Club's Roll of Honour for players only is as follows:-

> Alfred E. Briggs, 16th Royal Scots
> James Boyd, Do. Do.
> Patrick Crossan, Do. Do.
> Duncan Currie, Do. Do.
> Ernest E. Ellis, Do. Do.
> Norman Findlay, Do. Do.
> James H. Frew, 1st Lowland RGA

Thomas Gracie, 16th Royal Scots
James Low, Do. Do.
Neil Moreland, Argyll and Sutherland Highlanders
Annan Ness, 16th Royal Scots
Robert Preston, Do. Do.
George Sinclair, RFA
James H. Speedie, Cameron Highlanders
Henry Wattie, 16th Royal Scots
William Wilson, Do. Do.

In addition your Directors pledged themselves to raise for the 16th Royal Scots one full Company from the Club's supporters, and it is gratifying to record that for the record that the effort was more than accomplished. A Roll of Honour is being prepared for all those who specifically enlisted as supporters or members of the Club.

Another feature in the Club's anxiety to 'do it's bit' is the amount of money (£187, 13s 8d) it directly raised for the various War Funds. Also the Club and its players have taken a prominent part in the realisation of approximately £2,000 in aid of the Belgian Relief Funds here and in Glasgow.

Your Directors believe that the hearts of every patriot, sportsman and Club supporter go with the players in their new sphere of operations. That they may each return safe and sound, crowned in the laurels of victory, is the sincere wish of all. No club ever had control of a better or more loyal and anxious set of players. That they were a credit to Edinburgh and an example to all classes engaged in sport cannot be disputed.

On Thursday 8 July James Speedie, his Army training completed, embarked for France with the Queen's Own Cameron Highlanders. On landing at Boulogne the following day, he wrote to John McCartney informing his manager of his safe arrival.

On 29 July Ernie Ellis married his sweetheart Isobel Armstrong.

2

Season 1915/16

When the season commenced, the war was affecting everyone and attendances at games began to decline as the conflict was now biting deeply into everyday life. The Hearts side was made up of servicemen on leave and players engaged in vital war work such as Peter Nellies, who was a coal miner and worked in the mines in and around Douglas Water in Lanarkshire. All this put a drain on the energy of the players and with the constantly changing team selection, form varied from week to week. Hearts' season began on 21 August with a 4-1 defeat by St Mirren at Love Street. It was a very much changed team that took the field against St Mirren that Saturday, with only Archie Boyd, Harry Graham and Willie Wilson being regulars from the previous season's side. Bob Mercer had, however, returned to the team after being absent for almost a year through injury. Although Hearts had held their own in the first half, which had ended 1-1, slackness in the defence saw the 'Saints' score three more goals in a ten-minute spell. The Hearts line-up was: Boyd; Frew, J. Wilson; D. Graham, Mercer, Martin; McEwan, Blackhall, Aitken, H. Graham, W. Wilson.

In their first home game the following week, Hearts recorded a 3-0 victory over Hamilton Academical. The newspapers of the day remarked that the win said a great deal about the young and inexperienced side, that they were able to produce such a good standard of very entertaining football throughout the game. The scribes also wrote that the young Hearts team had received tremendous backing and encouragement from the support within Tynecastle. This victory was followed up with a well-deserved 2-0 win over Partick Thistle at Firhill but a home defeat at the hands of Kilmarnock on 11 September brought the fans back to earth. Prior to kick-off, the 9,000 fans who had turned up were entertained by the pipe band of the 5th Royal Scots. Included in the spectators was a party of wounded soldiers from

Craigleith Military Hospital, who were given a warm ovation as they took their seats in the stand. However, the next three games played in September were more encouraging. Fine wins were recorded at Shawfield and Easter Road, when Clyde and Hibernian were beaten 4-1 and 2-1 respectively. The month ended with a 1-1 home draw with Airdrieonians in front of a crowd of 8,000.

Then came shattering news from France, which sent the players, management and support into deep despair. On the morning of 25 September the British Army mounted an offensive at Loos. It was the largest ever full-scale assault seen on the Western Front in 1915. Advancing over open fields, with little or no cover, the British losses were devastating as the German machine guns and artillery cut them to pieces with withering fire. Among the fallen was James Speedie. He was twenty-one years of age. His tour of duty in France had lasted only eleven short weeks. The Saltire and the Union Flag flew at half-mast over Tynecastle.

Almost a month later, Tom Gracie died of leukaemia after being admitted to Stobhill Hospital in mid-September. Tom had been diagnosed with the illness some six months earlier but he had continued to play for the club he loved while at the same time carrying on his training with the Army. He had kept his secret from his teammates, telling only John McCartney of the problem. Quite simply, he should have remained at home in bed but Tom Gracie would not lie down to his illness, which must have taken exceptional courage.

On 26 October, Tom Gracie's funeral took place at Craigton Cemetery in Glasgow, within the shadow of Ibrox Park, a ground where only a year previously he had played a major part in Hearts' 2-1 defeat of Rangers in front of 41,000 spectators. John McCartney and Bob Mercer represented the directors and players respectively.

Following the funeral, and despite her grief, his mother took time to write a touching letter to John McCartney, saying that during his time at Tynecastle she had never seen her boy so happy and that Tom had found his home with Hearts. Harriet Gracie finished the letter to McCartney by thanking him for bringing her son to Edinburgh. Death had already visited the Gracie household a few weeks earlier. Mrs Gracie's other son, John, had died on 28 September 1915 as a result of wounds sustained at Loos on the opening day of the battle. Like James Speedie, he had served his country with the Queen's Own Cameron Highlanders.

James Speedie was the first Hearts player to be killed in action. Born at Leslie Place, Stockbridge, Edinburgh, on 17 November 1893, he was the younger of the two sons of John and Janet Speedie. He worked as an insurance clerk with the North British & Merchantile Marine Company and his footballing career began with Tranent Juniors. After playing as a trialist against Leith Athletic, Speedie signed for Hearts on an amateur contract on 28 May 1913. He made an impressive debut for Hearts on 16 August 1913, when he scored twice in a 3-1 win over Airdrieonians. It was his only League appearance that season as he was deputising for Willie Wilson. He made his breakthrough into the first team the next season, playing eight League games and scoring three goals in the process before going off to France.

James Speedie's body was never found. He is commemorated on the Loos Memorial at Dud Corner Cemetery, Loos, which was erected to the memory of the 20,000 officers and men who died in that area and have no known grave.

In October, John McCartney received a month-old censored letter from James Speedie. In the letter, James enquired as to the well-being of his team mates and asked the manager to pass on his best wishes to them. It was heart-breaking for McCartney as he read the contents over and over again as he tried to come to terms with the poignant note which had been signed simply 'James'.

In June 1917 John and Janet Speedie suffered more grief when their other son, John, lost his life while serving with the 4th Royal Scots in France. He was twenty-five years of age.

Following on from Tom's death, an article appeared in the Liverpool newspaper *Football Echo*, paying tribute to his time on Merseyside. Mrs Gracie penned a letter to the journalist at the newspaper in response to the very warm and sincere tribute he had paid to her son. The letter was published in full in the newspaper:

I have to thank you most sincerely for your article regarding my dear son, Tom. Tokens of respect such as you have written help to lighten the burden the loss of him is to us who loved him so much. Only God knows what I have lost in my darling boy, and when I state that another loved son of mine fell in battle on September 28, only three and a half weeks before Tom died, you will understand what my loss is, and how much I appreciate any little words of praise, especially coming from such an unlooked source as yours did. They who have gone have left pleasant memories behind them to others outside their own private circle. I would like to thank all Liverpool sympathisers – Mrs. Gracie.

It is hardly surprising that, on the playing front, the team's form was up and down. On 2 October a point was dropped after a 1-1 draw against Falkirk at Brockville and the week following, Ayr United dealt a further blow with a crushing 5-0 win at Tynecastle. The following fixture was Rangers away from home, and surprisingly the Maroons inflicted a 4-0 defeat on the Ibrox men, with Willie Wilson helping himself to a hat-trick. This was Rangers' first defeat of the season and it was suffered before an attendance in the region of 20,000. This vein of form continued during October with wins against Morton at home 2-0, and Motherwell 3-1 at Fir Park.

After twelve games, McCartney's ever-changing sides had recorded seven wins, two draws and suffered three defeats. They were second in the League to Celtic, although the Glasgow side had played two games less.

	Played	Won	Lost	Drawn	For	Against	Points
CELTIC	10	8	2	0	25	9	16
HEARTS	12	7	3	2	23	15	16
RANGERS	8	7	1	0	22	8	14

But attendances were falling all over Scotland, placing financial constraints on clubs. Hearts were no exception, with the result that the directors had to

Born in Glasgow in 1889, Tom Gracie signed for Hearts in May 1914, a month short of his twenty-fifth birthday. Tom was an old-fashioned centre forward who began his footballing career with Wellwood Star, a juvenile side from Glasgow's East End. In 1906 he transferred to Strathclyde FC, who at that time played in the Glasgow Junior League. In January 1907 he turned senior with Airdrieonians, playing against Queen's Park at the opening of the new stand at Broomfield. In 1908 he joined Lanarkshire rivals Hamilton Academical on 20 November, making his debut the following day against Third Lanark at Cathkin. He only made five appearances, scoring only a single goal, for the Douglas Park side before returning to Airdrie a few months later.

In September 1909 Tom was on his travels again, this time to Arthurlie, before being transferred to Greenock Morton on 24 May 1910. His next move took him further afield, when he travelled to Merseyside to join Everton on 27 March 1911. Tom spent less than a year at Everton before making the short trip across the way to sign for rivals Liverpool. He made 32 League appearances in a Liverpool jersey, making a scoring debut against Bury on 24 February 1912. But Gracie couldn't settle down in England and on 14 May he came 'back up the road' to Tynecastle. The shrewd John McCartney viewed Gracie as the last piece of the jigsaw of the great team he was assembling to challenge for honours in the Scottish game. He was proved correct when Gracie became an integral part of McCartney's team, becoming the leading Scottish goalscorer in the 1914/15 season. The loss of Tom Gracie, not yet at the summit of his career, was a terrible blow to everyone involved in the Scottish game.

Tom Gracie photographed at Tynecastle.

take a firm grip on expenditure. There was even an attempt to sell the 'Iron Stand' on the west side of the ground; it was quoted as suitable for 'a farm shed or a motor garage'. The local biscuit factory, McVittie & Price, offered £150 for the structure but this was thought to be insufficient and the offer was turned down. With a shortfall at the turnstiles, the club had to borrow from the bank in order to pay wages. Hearts were also well supported by their major creditors, J. Duncan & Sons and Redpath Brown Limited, who did not press for payment in respect of work to the stand until the war had ended.

In addition, Hearts had totally loyal and hardworking staff, particularly John McCartney, who worked tirelessly for the club and also looked after the interests of two cinemas, the Salon Picture House, situated at the top of Leith Walk, and the Tivoli in Gorgie Road. He managed both, being

The Heart of Midlothian board of directors. From left to right, standing: John McCartney, William Drummond and William Brown. Seated: William Lorimer, Elias Furst and William Burns.

responsible for the bookkeeping and virtually everything else that was required to run a cinema. Carrying out duties at the cinemas allowed McCartney to voluntarily reduce his salary at Tynecastle to £1 per week in an effort to reduce the wage bill at the club. He and his family resided in a club house in Moat Street, just of Slateford Road. His players on active service wrote to McCartney on a regular basis, keeping him informed of what was happening overseas. Although the contents of letters were censored by order of the Defence of the Realm Act, implemented in August 1914, John McCartney had a good idea of what life was like for his 'boys' on the front line and it worried him.

With what spare time he had left, McCartney was instrumental in organising 'Footballs For Soldiers', a charity designed to raise funds to enable footballs to be sent overseas for use by the troops. The project was a huge success and McCartney wrote the following tribute in his publication *The Hearts and the Great War* to the persons who had assisted and made it possible:

One thousand and seventy footballs have been despatched each accompanied by a covering letter. The cost of the administration is somewhere in the neighbourhood of one per cent.

Early in the war applications for footballs began to pour in at Tynecastle from the soldiers overseas, and from sailors of the Navy. The Club stock had been cleared – mostly to units training at home. Something had to be done to meet the demands of those on active service. The writer made an appeal through the columns of the *Edinburgh Evening News* and the Editor, in giving publicity to the letter, added a footnote suggesting that public subscriptions should be sent to Tynecastle, and that the business should be dealt with from there. The strong support of the *News* with one of its contributors (Diogenes) lending his hearty and strenuous aid, saw the scheme launched on a proper working basis.

It was fitting that the first subscription to the Fund should come from the *News* employees. That donation was the harbinger of a steady flow of revenue for the maintenance of the scheme. Individuals, corporations, public works – aye, even the soldiers themselves have vied with each other in their efforts of support. The incessant call of our heroes caught the ear of many outside Edinburgh. Substantial sums have come from London, Liverpool, Newcastle,

Glasgow, Paisley, Greenock, Leith, Kirkcaldy, Selkirk, Galashiels, Inverness, Rosyth, Pumpherston, Coldstream, Bathgate, Dunfermline, Gorebridge, Musselburgh, Slateford, Leven, Ormiston, Burntisland, Linlithgow, West Calder, Granton, Tranent, and a place, they call it – Drumnadrochit. The soldiers in France, friends in U.S.A. and West Africa added their quota. Just as the subscription field has been wide so has the distribution of the footballs. Practically every battalion in the British Forces has benefited. The soldiers of the French and the American Republics, and those of the Kingdoms of Belgium, Italy, Serbia and Greece have played with Tynecastle footballs. Members of the Canadian, Australian, South African, New Zealand and the Indian contingents have also participated in the benefits of the scheme. Letters from all ranks in the Allied Armies – the Allied Commander-in – Chief to the humblest Private – breathe grateful thanks and appreciation. Football was just the antidote the soldier required. We give quotations from several of the four thousand communications in our possession. These letters are in reality heart expressions of our fighting men addressed to a generous public, and we ask that they be read as such.

It is obviously impossible to quote even short extracts from all the letters in our possession but a selection at random will prove conclusively that football has played a great and important part in the history of the war. The entire stocks of tonic and reinvigorating nerve potions of the world's pharmacy fall into insignificance when compared with the stimulating football. The much discussed 'tot of rum' had no backers when football was about. Wearied and exhausted men, on their return to rest camps after long spells in the trenches were instantly revived by the sight of a ball. The filling of shell holes – hard and laborious work – became child's play in the formation of a pitch. The roar of guns and occasional shell visitors could not damp the ardour of these brave lads. Twenty players on each side and a game lasting four hours raised enthusiasm to a tremendous height. The gladiators fell asleep arguing the point and discussing incidents what time Fritz and Jerry were elaborating plans of murder and frightfulness. Comparison with the craven heart of a murderer, as against that of the buoyant sportsman is odious. The sporting instinct of the British soldier is an asset no laboratory of demonism could ever hope to counteract. Sportsmen – everyone a brother – make the world sublime and full of happiness, brightness and splendour, where only universal love and esteem may reign. The militarist, with his engines of destruction fetching death and desolation to mankind, produces but a vale of tears.

Among many letters of thanks received were ones from Marshal Foch, Commander-in-Chief of the Allied Armies; the King of Belgium; Marshal Joffre, Commander-in-Chief of the French Army; and General Diaz, Commander-in-Chief of the Italian Army. There was even one from Alfie Briggs, who wrote of his joy in being able to play a game of football again, even though he was playing in Army boots, and keeping up his levels of fitness.

The letters were poignant and touching, especially the one from Alfie Briggs. McCartney was moved by the number of them received at Tynecastle but he was stung by the level of criticism the scheme had received from some quarters and so further wrote:

These extracts we affirm, are conclusive proof of the efficacy of football. As already indicated, the quotations are but a mere fraction of the grand total. Many of them bear the signatures of from one to eighty men, thus implying, by a moderate estimate, that thousands have been cheered and gladdened through the Tynecastle fund. The cheerfulness has not been all on one side, for have not the kind hearts at home been equally just as pleased to find the necessary capital. To the eternal credit of the citizens and district friends they saw to it that Jack and Tommy were assured of their footballs.

We have critics who suggest that too much has been made of this element of sport in relation to the fighting man. With the exception of the effeminate curate they belong to the exclusive set of elderly sixties and youthful seventies who frolic and gambol in the aristocratic parlour at ping pong, or become breezy over an exciting tidley-wink contest. They pull crackers for exercise, and wear paper hats as a preventitive to ice rinks forming on their domes. Seriously speaking these dismal Jimmies have only one fighting garment – sack cloth and ashes. Youthful exuberance fired with zeal, energy, and exercise can alone win the war. The athlete you simply cannot subdue. The phlegmatic is beaten before he commences. Contributors to the Fund are numbered by the thousand. The administrators are profoundly grateful for the valuable assistance of the many voluntary workers, and keenly appreciate the kindness of every individual who helped even to the matter of a single penny.

McCartney then went on to list a number of people, including principal subscribers to the fund, the female collectors at the football matches, boys and girls who had provided back-court concerts, who had all worked hard to realise the sums of money raised. But there was one particular tribute that John McCartney paid that is worth mentioning as it describes perfectly the spirit and resilience of the people at home.

> Private R.C.F. Hyslop, Canadian Infantry, now resident at 5, Harrison Road, Edinburgh has proved himself a superb worker. Invalided out of the Colonial Forces as physically unfit, he set himself to do what he could from the confines of his little wheel-chair. The football instinct was strong within him, and he knew exactly the soldiers' sedative. He is a familiar figure sitting at the door of his home with his 'Football for Soldiers' collection box beside him, the while he is writing letters and sending subscription sheets broadcast. His total of £182,18s. 5d includes sums from Colonial Premiers and Statesmen. Amongst the public works and various business concerns he has been most successful. His inestimable services can hardly be measured in words. Private Hyslop, despite his serious handicap, has done magnificently. He holds a firm place in the hearts of all – soldier and administrator alike.

John McCartney finished by saying, 'After reading the particulars herein set forth, who can gainsay but that there is a close affinity between His Majesty's Forces and the Heart of Midlothian Football Club – a connection that will be remembered and recounted with pride in the decades to come.'

How prophetic that simple, but beautifully worded last sentence came to be.

Various other citizens of Edinburgh did their bit for the war effort. Alex Sim founded the Scottish Veterans' Garden City Association under the chairmanship of Lord Salvesen. Mr Sim was a property owner who, along with a group of professional people, paid for the construction of houses for the use of wounded servicemen.

Jimmy Duckworth played his part to the full. He bravely battled on with his various and numerous tasks at Tynecastle while never having recovered fully from the pneumonia he had contracted while accompanying the men on their marches in the Pentland Hills; and of course the support, who continued to turn up at Tynecastle in good numbers to pay their money at the turnstiles and to encourage the makeshift Hearts sides that McCartney was forced to field. As was expected, the team's form was indifferent from one week to the other but on Saturday 13 November a surprise 2-0 defeat of Celtic at Tynecastle brought a smile back to the faces of the fans. The following is a report of the game from the *Edinburgh Evening News* which demonstrates the changes that have taken place over the years with regards to the style of match reporting:

Fifteen thousand spectators witnessed the Heart of Midlothian defeat the Celtic by 2 goals to 0 at Tynecastle, Edinburgh. It was an excellent game with both sides playing pretty football, but the Heart of Midlothian were the more deadly forward and won on their merits. Indeed, the margin in their favour might have been greater, for on at least three occasions the upright saved the Celtic goal. All the honours lay with the home team in the first half, but all their pressure yielded but one goal, W. Wilson cutting into the centre, and beating Shaw after two attempts. There was a strong revival on the part of the Celtic after the interval, and the home defence, in which Mercer played a steady game, was fully stretched. The Hearts survived all attacks and ten minutes from the close made the issue certain. W. Wilson broke away on the left, and from his centre Welsh scored. The Celtic had several chances near the finish, but none was accepted.

After that win the top of the League table was as follows:

	Played	Won	Lost	Drawn	For	Against	Points
RANGERS	10	9	1	0	31	8	18
CELTIC	12	9	3	0	28	12	18
HEARTS	14	8	4	2	25	16	18

It was at this point that Willie Wilson, the top goalscorer, having netted 12 goals in 15 games, left for the Army. He had volunteered earlier but Willie had a constant problem with his shoulder and as a result of this he was kept back in reserve until such time as it was deemed necessary for him to go.

In the early part of 1916 the availability of players was becoming a massive problem, placing a severe burden on McCartney and the remaining playing staff. The players serving in the forces were now all in France and could not be called upon. Elsewhere, other clubs were encountering problems in fielding eleven players. The manager of Hamilton Academical, Alec Raisbeck, was driven to ask permission to play for the 'Accies' in an emergency. Raisbeck, a former player with Partick Thistle, had his request granted.

Rangers were asked to explain why they fielded only nine players in a match against Falkirk. The Ibrox club explained that illness, injury, Government work and finally fog on the day of the game had deprived them of eight of the seventeen players they had available for the fixture. The fog had delayed some of the players arriving at Brockville.

The ongoing problem with players' availability eventually came to a head for Hearts in April, when, for the first time ever, they failed to fulfil a League fixture. The game scheduled to be played was against Morton at Greenock. Due to both problems with travel arrangements and Hearts not being able to raise a side 'worthy of the club', the game was cancelled. As it transpired, the result did not affect the League positions and the game was never played, with no action being taken against Hearts by the Management Committee. Both clubs completed thirty-seven fixtures against the rest of the League's thirty-eight. Hearts rounded off their League campaign with a 1-0 victory over Dundee at Tynecastle with the following line-up: A. Boyd; M. Keirnan, J. Wilson; F. Welsh, R. Mercer, P. Nellies; G. Sinclair, J. McEwan, J. Bell, H. Graham, J. Blackhall. A much changed side from that which began the season against St Mirren.

All things considered, Hearts did exceptionally well to finish joint-fifth in the League championship, which was eventually won by Celtic. It was interesting to note that Hearts' home attendances in the League for the 1915/16 season averaged 7,631.

Final League positions were:

	Played	Won	Lost	Drawn	For	Against	Points
CELTIC	38	32	3	3	116	23	67
RANGERS	38	25	7	6	87	39	56
GREENOCK MORTON	37	22	8	7	86	35	51
AYR UNITED	38	20	10	8	72	45	48
PARTICK THISTLE	38	19	11	8	65	41	46
HEART of MIDLOTHIAN	37	20	11	6	66	45	46

HAMILTON ACADEMICAL	38	19	16	3	68	76	41
DUNDEE	38	18	16	4	56	49	40
DUMBARTON	38	13	14	11	53	64	37
KILMARNOCK	38	12	15	11	46	49	35
ABERDEEN	38	11	15	12	51	64	34
FALKIRK	38	12	17	9	45	61	33
AIRDRIEONIANS	38	11	19	8	44	74	30
MOTHERWELL	38	11	19	8	55	81	30
CLYDE	38	11	20	7	49	71	29
THIRD LANARK	38	9	18	11	40	56	29
ST. MIRREN	38	12	22	4	50	67	28
QUEEN'S PARK	38	11	21	6	53	100	28
HIBERNIAN	38	9	22	7	44	71	25
RAITH ROVERS	38	9	24	5	30	65	23

But the quality of life on the home front for the families was becoming increasingly poor. The residents of Edinburgh had already been the victims of bombing raids by the Germans. On the night of 2/3 April 1916, two enemy Zeppelins dropped high explosive and incendiary bombs on the city. Among the areas affected were the Grassmarket, Lothian Road, the Castle Rock, the Mound and Leith. Eleven people were killed, many were injured and property received substantial damage. This treacherous act did nothing to affect the moral of the public, whose spirit remained strong and unstinting.

Changes were seen in Scotland's capital to help in the war effort. Part of Edinburgh Castle was converted into a sixty-bed military hospital. The fortress was equipped with all the amenities necessary for a war hospital, including an operating theatre.

Bangour Village Hospital, which lay some twenty miles west of Edinburgh in the village of Dechmont, West Lothian, became Edinburgh's War Hospital in 1915, when it was requisitioned by the Government. It had been officially opened in 1906 as a psychiatric hospital and had accommodation for up to 800 patients. By 1918, the number of war-wounded patients it could accommodate had risen to over 3,000 and prefabricated huts and temporary marquees were erected to deal with the demand for beds.

Harry Graham. An intelligent and skilful inside forward, Harry Graham was also a qualified dentist. He was born on 16 December 1886 at Tollcross, Edinburgh, and grew up an ardent Hearts fan. Although asthmatic, he was able to play football and appeared in the Junior Grade with Granton Oakvale. Hearts tried to sign him early in his footballing career, but Harry preferred to remain in the junior ranks, both to obtain junior international honours and to complete his dentistry qualifications. He was quick, mobile and deceptive and it was St Bernards that took him into the senior grade in November 1908. He was transferred to Bradford City in April 1910. Harry went to Birmingham FC (not City until 1946) the following season and then joined Raith Rovers in August 1912. He assisted the Fifers to the Scottish Cup final in April 1913 but lost out on a winner's medal as Falkirk took the trophy with a 2-0 win at Celtic Park.

John McCartney brought him to Tynecastle two months later for a then substantial fee of £200. Harry went on to play 174 games for his boyhood heroes, 146 of them being League appearances. Although his main role was to create chances, he also scored 66 goals, 47 in the Championship. In his first full season at Tynecastle, Harry scored 22 goals in all matches, winning three local cup medals. He then contributed 18 league goals in the ill-fated 1914/15 season.

However, like so many others, the war interrupted his playing career at its peak and even though he was exempt from service, due to his profession, Harry volunteered for the Army. During his initial training the asthma found him out and he transferred to the RAMC, where he served as a dental officer. He was sent with the Gloucester Regiment to France and then saw service in Greece and Russia. Harry returned from the war in August 1919 and on resuming playing found it difficult to regain a regular place in the team; in December 1920 he joined Leicester City. After short spells with St Bernards and Reading, he retired from the game in 1925. Harry Graham died on 1 March 1940.

James Low. A traditional-style winger, Jimmy Low's career was prematurely ended due to the injuries that he received on active service during the Great War. He was born in Kilbirnie, Ayrshire, on 9 March 1894 but was brought up in Elgin, where his father owned a fishing net factory. He was a potential star footballer with Elgin City and signed for Hearts in August 1912. This was a most welcome move as Jimmy was a student of agriculture at Edinburgh University and was spotted by John McCartney playing for the university's side, although still registered with Elgin City. He made a scoring debut when Hearts won 4-2 in a League match against Rangers at Ibrox on 21 September 1912. Jimmy immediately earned a regular first-team place with some dashing displays down the right wing and he also had an eye for a scoring chance. He won several local cups during his Tynecastle days: the North-Eastern Cup in 1912/13; the Wilson Cup, the East of Scotland Shield and the Rosebery Charity Cup in 1913/14; and the Wilson Cup, the East of Scotland Shield and the Dunedin Cup in 1914/15. Prior to his departure for the battlefields, Jimmy played twice for the Scottish League XI. He made 83 League and Cup appearances for Hearts, scoring 18 goals.

J. LOW

With most of his colleagues, Jimmy joined the 16th Royal Scots and quickly became a corporal. Because of his university education, he was wanted by a special operations group involved in gas warfare. He was not keen on this assignment and was able to remain on active service by securing a commission in the 6th Seaforth Highlanders, where he attained the rank of lieutenant. While on active service, Jimmy was twice wounded. On 14 April 1917 it was reported in *The Scotsman* that Lieutenant James Low, Seaforth Highlanders, had been wounded on the head. When he was discharged from the Army on 10 June 1918, he was physically disabled and Hearts eventually granted him a free transfer in May 1919. Thankfully, his injuries improved and by 1920 he was back playing for Elgin City. Incredibly, he was offered a trial with Hearts in March 1920 but decided to take up a similar offer with Rangers. He was signed by the Glasgow club and subsequently joined Newcastle United in October 1921. During his stay on Tyneside he helped United to win the FA Cup in 1924, when they beat Aston Villa 2-0 at Wembley.

On retirement in 1930, he returned to Elgin to run the family business. He lost his son, David, in the Second World War. James Low died on 5 March 1960 in Elgin.

Jamie Low in the uniform of the Seaforth Highlanders, pictured with Dr Chalmers, Medical Officer, and Sergeant McGillvray while recruiting in Glasgow.

Willie Wilson. One of Hearts' greatest wingers, Willie Wilson gave the club magnificent service from 1912 until 1923, scoring almost 100 goals in some 325 games. His record might have been even better, but unfortunately he was away for three years on active service during the war and was wounded at Arras in 1917.

Born a stone's throw from Tynecastle at McLeod Street in February 1894, it was always his dream to play for Hearts. Willie developed his game with Shaftesbury Juveniles and Brandon Juveniles before moving into the junior grade with Arniston Rangers, where he earned two junior international caps. In March 1912 his dreams came true when he signed for Hearts. He quickly established himself in the first team and although he could play most positions up front, John McCartney saw his true position as being out on the wing. Willie's wing wizardry soon caught the eye of the sporting public, who thought that it would be only a matter of time until he would be capped for his country. Only the famous Alan Morton of Rangers kept him out of the Scottish team, although Willie was selected to play for the Scottish League in 1914 against the Football League. Willie was one of the Hearts players who volunteered in November 1914 to serve in the war; however, he did not go to France with McCrae's Battalion due to sustaining a dislocated shoulder on the football field. Willie remained in Edinburgh with the Reserve Company but eventually went to France, returning home in 1917. As expected, the war had sapped some of his strength and pace and his form declined. Added to that, he was also handicapped by the regular dislocation of his shoulder. In July 1923 the club gave him a benefit match against an East of Scotland Select and in September of that year he signed for Cowdenbeath. When his footballing days came to an end, he moved to Stretford in Manchester to work at his trade as a tinsmith.

Willie Wilson passed away in 1955 in Cheshire.

Bangour Village Hospital Church was built between 1924 and 1930 and contains a memorial chapel to commemorate the part played by the hospital in treating and nursing back to health casualties of the Great War.

The North British Rubber Company situated at Fountainbridge manufactured, among other items, one million pairs of trench boots for use on the Western Front. Other factories began to be built or extended to supply the country with materials required for the war. The Summer Time Act of 1916 was passed by Parliament and on 21 May 1916 British Summer Time was introduced to save daylight, fuel and money. Germany had already put this into practice to assist its war effort.

Inflation was on the increase and many could not afford the steep rise in food prices. But the Heart of Midlothian football club looked after their own and from time to time McCartney would arrange for boxes of groceries to be delivered to the homes of players' families who were struggling to cope. Occasionally, an envelope containing some money would be slipped in along with the food.

Fuel was also in short supply and would eventually be subject to rationing as nearly everything was directed towards the war effort. The demand for

Bangour Village Hospital, photographed from the air.

Bangour Village Hospital church.

war materials resulted in factories and mines working all but round the clock to ensure that the war effort was maintained. It was left to women to take the place of the men who had gone off to war. The country's women had answered the Government's earlier appeal for women to be engaged in war work. Women had now taken up employment in munitions factories, agricultural work and in transport, driving buses, trams and taxi cabs. It spoke volumes for the many who still found the time and the money to continue making the effort to follow the fortunes of their side and keep the club alive.

But if the quality of life for those at home was poor, then the state of living for those on the Western Front was practically non-existent. People may well imagine that life for the men serving in France was filled with violent action, whether it was furious attacks or desperate defending. That was indeed the case on occasions but sometimes they took up no more than four or five days a year for the average soldier. The remainder of the time was spent in the tedious routine of trench warfare, living in conditions which beggared belief. The majority of trenches were muddy, cold and totally depressing.

The usual trench system had three lines of trenches, consisting of the front line, the support and the reserve. They were joined to each other by communication trenches and the entire system was entered from the rear by an access trench which was out of sight of the enemy, and so the trench cycle would begin. A battalion would serve in the front line followed by a stint in the support and then in the reserve lines. But in reality the cycle was determined by the necessities of the situation.

Living conditions on the front line for the ranks below officer level consisted of small holes dug into the ground or into the side of the trench – sometimes their only cover was a waterproof sheet. Although the officers had slightly better accommodation, it was minimal. The floor of the trenches was covered with wooden duckboards that could quickly become submerged in squelchy mud when surface water drained into them, caused by heavy rainfall. Occasionally, the trenches could be filled with water so deep that it came up to the soldiers' waists. Sanitation was a word only to be found in a dictionary. Food was mainly tinned bully beef and damp biscuits. Clothing was filthy and caked with mud.

Death was a constant companion in the trenches thanks to the incessant shell fire by the Germans and the ever present threat of the sniper's bullet. Many a young life had been lost on their first day in the trenches due to inexperience on their part and by the unerring accuracy of the sniper waiting for his opportunity to fire the fatal bullet on sighting a head showing above the parapet of the trench. The shelling was particularly nerve-wracking, with the deafening noises continually surrounding the ears of the troops. Few could remain calm under these circumstances and consequently many suffered mental breakdown. Many soldiers simply died from exposure to the cold as temperatures often fell well below zero in the dead of winter. Fingers and toes were lost to frostbite.

Not only did the filth and foul odour of human waste and decaying bodies contribute to the spread of disease, they also attracted rats. The trenches were infested with them, the two main types being the brown and the black rat. Both were hated by the soldiers but the brown rat was especially despised. They would feed off human remains, growing to the size of a cat. It was not uncommon for them to scamper across the men's faces in the dark as the soldiers tried to get a few hours' rest. It was a terrifying experience to be woken up from a fitful sleep by a rat crawling across your face and body. Various methods were used by the troops to rid their living quarters of the vermin: bayoneting, shooting and even clubbing them to death was tried, but to no avail. The rats continued to breed incessantly, spreading infection and contaminating food and adding to the misery of life in the trenches. There were other sources of infection to contend with, such as lice. They were an ongoing problem, breeding in the seams of filthy clothing, causing unbearable and constant itching to the wearer of the garments. Lice were also responsible for trench fever. This was a painful disease that suddenly began with severe pain, followed by a high fever. Away from this environment, it could take up to twelve weeks for men to regain full recovery. Horned beetles, large slugs and massive swarms of flies were everywhere.

The area between the British trenches and the ones occupied by the Germans was known as no man's land. The distance could range from several hundred yards to, in some cases, less than ten yards and was heavily defended by machine guns, artillery and riflemen on both sides. It was often covered with large swathes of barbed wire and crudely made but deadly land mines. It was also strewn with dead bodies. After an advance or indeed a retreat, the wounded and dying were left out there before, under the cover of darkness, the stretcher bearers could go out to bring them back in. The stretcher bearers were a breed apart. It took an exceptional type of courage to perform the duties they were asked to do. In the dark, they would crawl over the thousands of shell-holes in no man's land to find the wounded and bring them 'home' while all the time waiting for a sniper's bullet to bring them down. The dead were left. Bodies would lie in no man's land for a long time without burial. There was no time to bury the multitude of corpses and on some battlefields burials did not take place until after the war. The men from the Heart of Midlothian experienced the trauma of all of this, and their friends and family at home were in despair at the extent of their suffering.

3

The Somme, 1916

In late January the Hearts players in the 16th Royal Scots – Jimmy Boyd, Alfie Briggs, Paddy Crossan, Duncan Currie, Ernie Ellis, Jimmy Hazeldean, Edward McGuire, Annan Ness and Harry Wattie – had moved up to the front line near to the village of Bois Grenier. They took up positions there to 'learn the ropes' of trench warfare under bitterly cold conditions. No sooner had they arrived that the Germans began a heavy bombardment, with over 2,000 shells raining down on them. Their shelter from the shelling consisted of water-filled trenches with sandbags placed along the parapet. Learning the ropes came very quickly to the Tynecastle men as they sat in the foul-smelling mud, praying that the next shell to explode would be nowhere near them. The shelling was then replaced with machine-gun fire. Alfie Briggs wrote to McCartney, telling him of the constant noise of the enemy machine guns. Paddy Crossan also wrote to McCartney but his main concern was not the German gunfire straddling the parapet of the trenches but the many rats occupying them. And so it went on.

But the Hearts family at home had not forgotten their gallant men. Annan Ness received a massive parcel from his manager for distribution among the regiment, the contents of which make remarkable reading: 240 pairs of socks; 141 lb of black tobacco; 12 fiddles; 100 boxes of Edinburgh Rock; 400 bars of Fry's milk chocolate; 300 candles; 20 cases of toilet soap; 12 dozen writing pads; 3,000 envelopes; 14 pairs of football boots; 3 balls; 2 pumps; assorted magazines and books and 1 melodeon. The melodeon, which was somewhat ironically made in Germany, was for Paddy Crossan. McCartney, it appeared, had not lost any of his subtle humour, his letter ending with the tongue-in-cheek 'I hope this will suffice, should you require anything else please to not hesitate to ask'.

Annan Ness's reply showed that he was not devoid of humour either.

Most of our time is spent digging holes in France to fill other holes in other bits of France. Much of the country is now contained in sandbags. The rest is in our boots, our pockets, our rifles and claret thick all over our uniforms. We are not at all the smart battalion you remember. Yesterday we built a road up to a trench on our front line, nothing very rugged, just a wooden planked affair. Today the Germans shelled it, so this evening we must start again. Still we can smile through the grime. One of the boys has just sent a parcel of mud home to his folks, together with instructions on how much water they must add in order to achieve the correct 'trench consistency'. Oh we have all the wags out here, all right.

Annan's letter must have brought a smile to the faces of John McCartney and Jimmy Duckworth's faces. The boys were still in great spirits.

In May the regiment moved to La Boiselle at the Somme, where they occupied the front line, familiarising themselves with the surrounding areas and the maze of trenches. Night raids were carried out into the enemy lines in order to glean information as to the German fortifications and their strengths in preparation for the forthcoming 'big push'.

In early 1916 the Allies were hopeful of bringing an end to the war by the late summer. The major military powers of the Alliance comprised of France, Great Britain, Italy and Russia. They were hoping to launch simultaneous attacks from three sides in an effort to gain victory and bring closure to the fighting. Planning was already in the advanced stages and the attacks were to be launched as early as possible in the summer. The joint British and French assaults were to be made side-by-side on the Somme. The Battle of the Somme began on 1 July and ended on 18 November 1916. Intended to be a major breakthrough, it became instead a byword for indiscriminate slaughter.

For a week before the attack commenced, the Allied artillery had pounded the German lines relentlessly, firing over a million and a half shells, to ensure a rapid advance. In other words, the underbelly of the German fortifications would be 'softened up', allowing the Allied advance to be virtually unhindered. That was the thinking of the High Command.

However, the Germans had other thoughts. Unconcealed preparations for the attack and the non-stop bombardment only served to give the enemy clear warning of what was about to take place.

Bob Preston photographed with James Boyd. Bob Preston was signed by John McCartney in August 1914 from Bathgate FC as cover for the injured Bob Mercer. Before he could make any impact at Hearts, Bob enlisted with his teammates in November that year, joining the Royal Scots. However, he spent most of his two and a half years' service with the Highland Light Infantry. At the cessation of hostilities, Bob returned home in January 1919. He

was found to be 2 stone heavier after military service but he trained hard and eventually was rewarded with a regular place in the first team, where he became the mainstay and prop of the defence. For his services he was awarded a Testimonial against Leeds United in 1921. In March 1922 he was disgracefully barracked by a section of the support at Tynecastle and his confidence suffered. In August, after 147 League and Cup appearances, he transferred to Torquay United in the Southern League. The change seemed to suit Bob and his form improved to the extent that Plymouth Argyle signed him in May 1923. He went onto play around 150 games for them before returning to Torquay United. When his playing days ended he moved to Northern Ireland, where he ran a pub in County Antrim and in the early thirties returned to football as the manager of Distillery. Bob Preston died in May 1945.

James Boyd. Born on 14 November 1894, James Boyd was brought up in the small village of Mossend, West Calder. He was educated at West Calder Public School and on finishing his education began work as a mine weighman at the oil works. James first played football with local juvenile side Mossend Burnvale and from there signed for Hearts on 22 August 1914, joining his brother Archie, who was already a goalkeeper at Tynecastle. John McCartney had high hopes for the youngster but due to the war, James never had the opportunity to make the first team, enlisting in November 1914.

James Boyd was killed on 3 August 1916 and although his body was found and buried in a rough grave, the ground was ploughed inch by inch by shell fire as the fighting continued and the exact location was lost. He was twenty-one years of age.

James is commemorated on the Thiepval Memorial to the Missing.

In 2012 a play, *The Scarf*, which was written in memory of James Boyd by ardent Hearts fan Sandy Potter, was first performed by the pupils of West Calder High School. The performance received great acclaim and since then *The Scarf* has played to sell-out audiences throughout West Lothian, a fitting tribute to the memory of a brave man.

Alfie Briggs photographed with Harry Wattie. Alfie Briggs was a Glasgow man, born in the Milton area of the city on 4 February 1888. On leaving school he worked as a machine builder at the Singer Sewing Works and played his football with Clydebank Juniors. In October 1912, Alfie was chosen to play in the Scotland *v.* Wales Junior International at Tynecastle. Such was his performance in the game that he was signed by Hearts later that month. He was a fine young half-back who, like so many others, never achieved his true potential due to the war. Alfie played 76 games for Hearts and scored only one goal, but he was a great club man, solid and reliable, and continued to support the team after he was forced to retire from the game. He did some scouting for Partick Thistle and went to work as a boiler maker. Alfie Briggs passed away on 18 March 1950 at the age of sixty-two.

A souvenir postcard of the Hearts players serving overseas. 1. Gracie; 2. Currie; 3. Wattie; 4. Crossan; 5. Frew; 6. Sinclair; 7. Findlay; 8. Ness; 9. Briggs; 10. Ellis; 11. Speedie; 12. Ellis; 13. Low.

Harry Wattie. Born Henry Benzie Wattie, Harry was brought up in the Meadows district of Edinburgh. He attended Boroughmuir High School and then became a clerk with an insurance company.

He grew up supporting Hearts and signed for them in August 1913 from Tranent Juniors. He was a quick, opportunist goalscorer and midfield general, scoring 17 goals in 58 League and Cup matches for the club. But like the others, his career was cut short when he volunteered to serve his country, joining the 16th Royal Scots. Harry Wattie's young life came to an abrupt end at the Somme Offensive on 1 July 1916. His body was never found and he is commemorated on the Thiepval Memorial to the Missing. Harry was twenty-five years of age.

The German trenches were not just heavily fortified; they were well equipped in comparison to the ones that housed the British. Underground dug-outs had been constructed under their trenches, protecting them from British shell-fire. When the shelling began the Germans simply moved underground and waited.

The advance was scheduled for 0730 hours on 1 July.

As the time drew nearer, some began to complete the 'Short Form of Will' which was to be found on page 12 of their Pay Books. Harry Wattie left everything to his mother, but by contrast Duncan Currie informed his father that there was no need to make a will as he would be coming home. Ernie Ellis, who was now the proud father of a baby daughter named Kitty, wrote to his wife Isobel saying how much he was looking forward to coming home to Edinburgh and seeing both of them. Ernie had still to set eyes on his daughter of a few months. He never would.

Many of the men spent a restless and sleepless night but those who did manage some rest woke on 1 July to a beautiful summer's morning as the sun broke over the horizon. The birds were singing clearly as they swooped and hovered over the lines of trenches, but it was not a sunrise worth waiting for. At 6.25 a.m. that peaceful and tranquil scene was cruelly interrupted by the British artillery beginning their intensive bombardment of the German positions. Yet again, when the shelling commenced, the Germans simply moved underground and waited ... the clock was ticking.

Most of the Hearts lads were together, except Annan Ness and Jimmy Boyd, who were at Company HQ. Paddy Crossan, Harry Wattie and Jimmy Hazeldean sat side by side, and for once the irrepressible Paddy was quiet. Nearby were Duncan Currie, Alfie Briggs, Edward 'Teddy' McGuire and Ernie Ellis, all understandably deep in thought. Their thoughts would have been of their loved ones and families back home in Scotland. Their thoughts would also have been of what fortune lay ahead in the day stretching before them. A day on which some of them would not see the sun set. The nervous tension was all around them. They watched quietly as some members of the regiment knelt down in silent prayer – God seemed very near to them at this time. Others were gazing at photographs of their families, which they touchingly kissed before returning them to the safety of the breast pocket of their tunics.

The British bombardment intensified, then at 7.28 a.m. two large mines either side of the main road at La Boisselle were detonated. They were intended to blow up the German trenches but fell short of their target and the German front line was still intact. Two minutes later, an eerie silence descended over the battlefield as British guns ceased their onslaught. By a strange coincidence, almost at the same time, the Germans' weaponry stopped firing. The sun shone out of a cloudless sky; and then, the serenity of the moment was gone.

The officers' whistles were blown and the advance 'over the top' began. They rose as one to the sound of the pipes playing 'Dumbarton's Drums'. Further along the lines, the 'Bluebells o'er the Border' was being played by a lone piper. The Battle of the Somme was underway.

They advanced slowly over no man's land towards the enemy lines, looking to left and right as if correcting their dressing on a parade ground, to where the Germans lay in wait. The barbed wire enforcements, which were supposed to have been blown away, were still in situ. Then the enemy's wait was over. They opened up with deadly fire from their machine guns and soon found easy targets as the advancing troops tried to find gaps in the wire. The Germans had also carried out their homework of the area. They had spotted the breaks in the barbed wire and very quickly turned the narrow passageways into death-traps with relentless and clinical firepower. The enemy did not need to take aim – they just pointed the guns and kept their fingers on the trigger. It became a slaughter as the gaps quickly filled up with the bodies of the dead and wounded. There was nowhere to go. Men fell where they stood as the murderous fire continued unabated. One young soldier was seen putting his hands in front of his face as if to shield himself from the withering fire. He was cut to pieces. As many died on the barbed wire as on the ground. Like fish caught in a net, they hung there in grotesque postures. They had died on their knees and the wire had prevented their fall; They looked as if they were in prayer. The whole scenario was heart-breaking. It was a living hell. There are no words adequate enough to describe it in its entirety.

Alfie Briggs was caught in the sights of a machine gun. Bullets raked his body, one breaking his right leg, another his left foot, another went through his right arm, another through his right ankle and the last one mercifully glanced him on the forehead, rendering him unconscious as he fell to the ground.

Flying shrapnel struck Teddy MacGuire and, as he began to fall, machine-gun fire grazed his head. Jimmy Hazeldean was shot in the thigh. Duncan Currie and Harry Wattie were cut down by machine-gun fire and died instantly. The slaughter continued. Ernie Ellis was next to suffer the fate which had already befallen his Tynecastle teammates, Duncan Currie and Harry Wattie. As the machine guns spat out their deadly fire, Ernie fell just in front of the barbed wire, his body riddled with bullets. Like many other children from the Great War, little Kitty Ellis would never know her father. Paddy Crossan was running forward when a shell exploded in front of him, causing a massive hole. He went down into the shell-hole and was covered under a large pile of earth and debris.

Little could be done for the many lying wounded out there in no man's land at that time. Many of the stretcher bearers following in the wake of the advancing troops had themselves become casualties. Thousands of wounded men out there took cover in shell holes or lay out in the blistering heat of the sun, unable to move due to the severity of the injuries they had sustained. Alfie Briggs, Teddy McGuire and Jimmy Hazeldean were among the number who were sheltered. Paddy Crossan was lying sheltered, although somewhat fortuitously. Of the ones lying badly wounded, many bled slowly to death or died from extreme shock; their cries for help simply could not be answered. It still wasn't 9 a.m. and already thousands had been killed. The German machine guns and snipers continued to wreak havoc on literally anything that moved throughout the rest of the day until thankfully dusk came.

Then it was time for the stretcher bearers to get to work as they set out to locate the wounded and bring them back safely to their own lines of defence under the cover of darkness. Briggs and McGuire were among the many brought back to have their wounds attended to by medical staff. Doctors and nurses were already overrun by the sheer volume of casualties being brought to the makeshift hospitals. The hospitals were either hastily put together tents or requisitioned buildings which were squalid and full of injured men, patiently waiting their turn. The workload of the doctors and nursing staff was phenomenal as they worked non-stop, attending to young men who were in severe and agonising pain. Quick decisions had to be made as to whether a life was worth saving or not. If a surgeon decided a badly wounded soldier was a hopeless case, the unfortunate soul was left to die while the medical staff concentrated on those who, in their view, had a better chance of survival. Amputation of limbs was commonplace; it was easier to take of a man's foot, leg or arm than operate to save them. And the wounded and dying kept on arriving. The surgeons, quite frankly, were overrun and were carrying out their work in conditions that were horrendous.

This is when the nursing staff played their part. They would comfort the dying and gently tell them that the wounds sustained weren't too serious and that soon they would be going home to be with their families and loved ones. Some of the severely wounded and broken men cried uncontrollably, unable to comprehend what was happening to them. Young boys lay cradled in the arms of the nurses, some barely older than themselves, before passing on to the arms of God. Her duty done, the nurse would quietly move on to the next man who was in need of loving and tender care before he too slipped away and found peace in death. For the many thousands, death was sometimes a welcome relief. It took a different type of courage to perform the duties that these 'angels' were asked to carry out. No stress counselling existed back then. It was your job and in simple terms, you just got on with it. How apt and somewhat ironic it was that a popular romantic song of the time was 'If you were the only girl in the world'.

Elsie Inglis, a graduate of Edinburgh University, formed the Scottish Women's Hospital and had already set up fourteen hospitals on various fighting fronts, which included the Somme. She was a formidable character who would not take 'no' for an answer. It was Elsie who first suggested that teams of women doctors and nurses be sent to the Western Front to assist with the casualties. Someone from the War Office replied, in rather pompous terms, 'My good lady, go home and sit still.' This reply was totally ignored by Elsie, who set about raising funds to enable the forming of the medical units which provided much-needed care for the soldiers serving overseas. Unfortunately this brave lady, who was 'hands on' with her teams of nurses, was unable to see out the war years. Elsie Inglis died of cancer in November 1917 and was laid to rest in Dean Cemetery, Edinburgh.

Winston Churchill said of Elsie and her nurses: 'They will shine in history.' The then Secretary of State for Foreign Affairs, Arthur Balfour, added his own tribute: 'Elsie Inglis was a wonderful compound of enthusiasm, strength of purpose and kindliness. In the history of this World War, alike by what she did and by the heroism, driving power and the simplicity by which she did it, Elsie Inglis has earned an everlasting place of honour.' In 2009 Elsie Inglis was commemorated on a new series of banknotes issued by the Clydesdale Bank. Her image appeared on the new issue of £50 notes.

Alfie Briggs benefited from the medical staff's dedication. Alfie was found in a shell-hole. Drenched in his own blood and in tremendous pain, he was brought to a field hospital. After a visual examination, he was placed in a tent and left after being deemed a 'hopeless' case. Extremely weak from loss of blood, Alfie fell into a deep sleep and would surely have died but for the alacrity of a hospital orderly. Several hours had passed when the orderly noticed that Alfie was still breathing and still very much alive. His condition was quickly reassessed and incredibly, after surgery, he survived and was shipped back to Britain for further treatment and recuperation. Teddy McGuire was stretchered back from the front and after treatment was also sent home.

Jimmy Hazeldean, with the help of another member of the regiment, arrived back at base. He, too, was eventually sent back to the UK for more surgery and later invalided out of the British Army along with Teddy MacGuire and Alfie Briggs.

Jimmy Hazeldean, who was from Alloa, had joined Hearts in August 1915 from Portobello Thistle Juniors. He played five League games before following the example of the other players and enlisting. After recovering from his injuries, he was re-registered by Hearts in August 1918. Sadly, Jimmy was unable to recover his form and was released by Hearts in April 1919 after playing one first-team game. This was in a 3-3 draw with a Canadian XI on 2 January 1919. Jimmy returned to his home town to work as a bottle-blower in a bottle factory but he kept his connection with the club, becoming a member of Hearts' Former Players Club. Jimmy died in 1980, another player whose full potential wasn't realised due to the Great War.

For hundreds of thousands of the wounded, the war never really came to an end. They had recurring nightmares and experienced flashbacks for years to come. One of them who suffered was Alfie Briggs. He was in pain for the remainder of his days and had to contend with bouts of depression, more so on the anniversary of the Battle of the Somme and Remembrance Day.

Paddy Crossan, Duncan Currie, Ernie Ellis and Harry Wattie were still unaccounted for and were feared dead. Then, on 8 July, a minor miracle occurred: Paddy Crossan wandered back into the regiment's camp to tell an amazing tale of survival. After being buried as a result of the German shell exploding beside him, he had regained consciousness the day after. Although badly concussed, Paddy had painstakingly crawled for three days towards the British lines before he was found. He was taken to a dressing station and treated before returning to his unit. His vision had been impaired as a result of the concussion but it had not affected his memory as he recounted his remarkable journey back to his lines and the horror he had encountered while crawling from shell-hole to shell-hole: holes that were occupied by countless corpses and the remains of bodies. On learning the fate of his

Patrick James Crossan was born in May 1893 in the village of Addiewell, just a few miles along the road from where Archie and James Boyd resided at Mossend, West Calder. Pat, or Paddy, was an explosive talent, a quick, robust and industrious full-back who became one of the most famous players to have worn a maroon shirt. This was not only because of his exploits on the field, but because he was also one of the volunteers who joined McCrae's Battalion in November 1914. He was recruited from the junior side Arniston Rangers in November 1911. Paddy was a popular member of the squad when Hearts first toured abroad in 1912 and 1914, and this fine defender also helped the team to reach the 1913 Scottish Cup semi-finals. He played for the Scottish League against the Southern League and his heroic war service at the peak of his career almost certainly cost him full international caps.

He made a remarkable recovery from all the injuries he sustained during the war. The redoubtable defender left the Army in January 1919 and returned to Tynecastle and remained a first-choice defender for Hearts until April 1925. Sadly, Paddy earned no major club honours but there were many happy memories and he gained thirteen local cup winners' medals. In addition, Hearts awarded him two Testimonial matches, against a Scotland XI in August 1920 and then against Manchester United in April 1924. In August 1925 Paddy travelled across the city to Leith to play for Leith Athletic but only remained there for a short period. In 1926 Paddy married Alice Wattie, the sister of Paddy's former teammate, Harry. He opened his famous Paddy's Bar in Rose Street and liked nothing better than to stand at the bar and have a 'good blether' with the patrons who frequented it. Paddy had many stories to tell.

On 28 April, Paddy Crossan passed away at the age of thirty-nine years, due in no small measure to his wartime experiences. He died at Southfield Sanatorium, Liberton, as a result of pulmonary tuberculosis (infection of the lungs).

On the day of his funeral, a huge crowd turned out at Mount Vernon Cemetery, Edinburgh, to pay their respects and say farewell to one of Heart of Midlothian's most wholehearted players and the 'handsomest man' in Scottish football.

It was said that he liked a 'small refreshment or two'; if ever a man deserved to partake of a drink, it was Patrick James Crossan.

Hearts teammates, Crossan knew that he was one lucky young man to be alive.

The body of Duncan Currie was found and buried in a rough grave in a battlefield plot near to the La Boisselle–Contalmaison Road. Ernie Ellis and Harry Wattie had simply disappeared. It is thought that when Gordon Dump Cemetery was formally laid out, the remains of Duncan Currie were interred there and that he is one of the unknown soldiers buried in that resting place.

The grim news of the tragic events in France was received stoically by McCartney; it was the news he had always dreaded. Jimmy Duckworth was inconsolable at the loss of 'his boys', and the happenings that had taken place in a country far from Tynecastle were soon to have a detrimental effect on his health. The directors, players and supporters of Heart of Midlothian were devastated by the impact. A city mourned and a nation wept for them, united in grief. The conciliatory telegrams and letters soon began to arrive at Tynecastle.

Families in Edinburgh, Fife and throughout the Lothians began to receive the brief and dreaded Army Form B. 104-82 beginning: 'It is my painful duty to inform you that ...' Isobel Ellis had just returned to her home at 25 Tarvit Street. She had been out in the nearby Meadows, taking a stroll with Kitty in the warm sun that was shining over Edinburgh that morning. The letter was waiting for them. Kitty was lying content and happy in her pram when her mother opened Form B. 104-82. No words can describe the grief that followed. Barely eighteen years of age and already widowed, with a young child to bring up, Isobel Ellis sobbed uncontrollably.

It wasn't until 1917 that the remains of her husband were found and buried but due to the ongoing conflict and mayhem the exact location of Ernie's grave was lost.

House number 12 in Marchmont Road, Edinburgh, had the same Form B delivered to the occupants, Mr and Mrs Wattie. Their son's body was never found; and so it went on.

The hostilities were still ongoing in France. On 3 August, Annan Ness received an injury to his arm from a piece of German shrapnel as the shelling continued. He had his wound dressed and simply carried on. Jimmy Boyd wasn't so fortunate. He was badly wounded in the same bombardment and was placed on a stretcher to be taken to a dressing station near to Bazentin-le-Petit. The stretcher party set off with Jimmy as the shelling intensified. They never reached their destination as another German shell did its deadly work, killing them outright. Jimmy's remains were found and buried but,

Duncan Currie. Duncan was an Ayrshire man, born on 13 August 1892 at 18 Double Row, Eglinton Iron Works, near Kilwinning. He was an assistant hairdresser in his brothers' hairdressing business and began his footballing career with the local junior side, Kilwinning Rangers. Heart of Midlothian signed him on 11 April 1912 for the sum of £2 2s. Duncan was a strong and resolute player who was comfortable playing in the left-back or centre half position and quickly became a regular in the first team, playing 45 League games and thirteen others in local cup competitions. It soon became clear that Hearts had discovered a player of great quality who was a born leader on the football field and international honours beckoned. But it was not to be as he volunteered for service in the 16th Royal Scots along with his colleagues.

Duncan's undoubted leadership skills were recognised in the Army and he attained the rank of sergeant. He fell while leading his platoon at the Somme Offensive on 1 July 1916 at the age of twenty-four. His name joined those of Ellis, Wattie and Boyd on the Thiepval Memorial to the Missing.

Above left: Duncan Currie photographed in the Hearts strip

Above:
Ernie Ellis
photographed at
Tynecastle.

Ernest Ellis. Ernie was from the Norfolk village of Sprowston, near Norwich. He became a boot clicker (he cut the upper part of the boot) by trade before becoming a professional footballer. He was a powerful defender who began his career at Norwich City before moving to Barnsley. Playing in the right-back position, he began to turn in some impressive performances, resulting in John McCartney moving for his signature on 16 May 1914 for the reported sum of £50. His first-team appearances were limited and the advent of war prevented him from making an impact.

Ernie's body was found and buried but, as was the case with his team mate James Boyd, the location was lost on the battlefield.

Ernest Edgar Ellis is commemorated on the Thiepval Memorial to the Missing.

as was the case with Ernie Ellis, the location of his grave was also lost in the carnage that was the Somme.

A few days after Jimmy Boyd's death, another blow was suffered by the Hearts contingent. A shell exploded near to Paddy Crossan, resulting in several pieces of shrapnel becoming embedded in his left leg. A shard of shell casing also penetrated his left foot, almost taking off his toes. He was removed to a field hospital, where he lost consciousness. When he came round again, Paddy noticed that someone had pinned a label on to his muddied and bloodied uniform. The label contained the message 'for amputation'. The doctors had decreed that Crossan's left leg was coming off. We can only imagine what was going through his mind at that time. His leg, which had made so many interventions and fearless tackles on opponents all over Scotland, was being taken away. Paddy Crossan, at twenty-two years of age, often described jokingly by his Tynecastle colleagues as the 'handsomest man in the world', was now seeing his world crashing all around him.

Then fate stepped in, in the unlikely shape of a German. A captured enemy soldier had been put to work in the hospital as an orderly but in reality he had been a surgeon in Germany before the outbreak of the war. The German informed the medical staff that amputation of the limb wasn't necessary as a simple operation would suffice and that he was prepared to carry it out. A decision was made, one, for once, that Paddy wasn't disputing, and the kindly enemy surgeon was allowed to operate. The operation was a success. Crossan must have been shaking hands with himself. It was one of the few times in this horrible war that the Heart of Midlothian had received 'the rub o' the green'. It was long overdue. Paddy was sent to Stourbridge Hospital in the West Midlands to recover and it was from there that he wrote to his manager. With typical self-belief, Paddy confidently informed John McCartney that he would soon be kicking a ball again. It was Crossan at his best – you just couldn't keep him down for any great length of time.

The Somme Offensive was an unmitigated disaster. On the first day alone, the British had lost 20,000 men killed, with casualties thought to be in the region of 40,000. By November 1916 that number had risen dramatically and even to this day the numbers thought to have been killed or wounded vary between 420,000 and 600,000. The exact numbers remain unknown.

Hot attack on Hearts' goal at Love Street. Boyd, Hearts' goalie, just clear a from Bruce, a St Mirren forward.   Frew, of Hearts, clearing from Bruce, St Mirren.

Two photographs from Hearts' opening League game of the 1915/16 season, against St Mirren at Love Street, showing Archie Boyd, the Hearts goalkeeper, clearing from James Bruce, the St Mirren forward; and Jimmy Frew clearing from the same player.

HEARTS WHO KNOCKED RANGERS KICKING.

Above left: It's half-time in the Rangers *v.* Hearts League game at Ibrox on 22 October 1915 and Hearts are ahead 1-0. From left to right: John MacKenzie, John Wilson, Jimmy Duckworth, Bob Mercer, Peter Nellies, George Miller, George Sinclair, Harry Graham, Archie Boyd, Willie Wilson and Fletcher Welsh. James Martin, who played left-half in the game, is missing from the photo. A further two goals from Willie Wilson and a late counter from Fletcher Welsh sealed the victory. The players often remained on the pitch at half-time due to fading light and to save time to ensure that certain train times could be met.

Above right: Duncan Currie, Paddy Crossan, Annan Ness and Harry Wattie photographed on the terracing at Tynecastle in 1914.

Opposite: Roll-call on the Somme on the morning of 1 July 1916. (J&C McCutcheon Collection)

Action from the Partick Thistle *v.* Hearts game on 4 September 1915 sees Harry Graham of Hearts heading for the Thistles goal. Hearts won the match 2-0, with goals from Willie Wilson and Tom Hamilton in front of a crowd of 14,000.

4

Season 1916/17

The overall depression caused by the calamitous events in France reflected on the team's performance during the season of 1916/17. Attendances at football grounds throughout the country continued to fall and the introduction of the Entertainment Tax by the Government did nothing to help the financial plight of many clubs, including Hearts.

Hearts' financial problems weren't helped by a protracted, and sometimes unpleasant, dispute over monies owed to them by Chelsea regarding the transfer of a player, Lawrence Abrams. Hearts had signed Abrams in 1910 from Stockport County and he proved to be a valuable asset to the club, making 157 appearances for the Gorgie side. However, in the 1913/14 season he expressed a desire to return down south to continue his footballing career. As Hearts required funds to finance the building of their new Main Stand, letters were sent offering his transfer to the leading Football League clubs. Chelsea recruited Abrams in June 1914 for the then substantial fee of £1,000 and initially gave Hearts £250, leaving an unpaid balance of £750 to be paid at a later date. Although numerous pieces of correspondence were sent to the London club, the balance remained unpaid, and subsequently Hearts obtained a court order in August 1916 to retrieve the £750. But Chelsea had absolutely no money in the bank – the club were completely broke. After a heartfelt appeal to Hearts by the Football League on behalf of Chelsea, the Edinburgh club did not pursue the matter any further and the Londoners were saved from going out of the game completely. If any club understood the problems being faced by all the clubs, it was Hearts.

On Saturday 19 August, Hearts' season began with a trip to Cappielow and this time McCartney was able to field eleven players. Again, it was a much-changed side from the one that had defeated Dundee in the last game of the previous season.

Hearts lined up: W. Black; M. Keirnan, J. Wilson; J. Laidlaw, R. Mercer, T. Ross; P. White, G. P. Miller, G. Noble, G. Boag, J. McEwan.

The side was largely of an experimental nature, containing several new players, and it showed as the forward line displayed a lack of cohesion and understanding in the opening stages. Morton took the lead after fifteen minutes but straight from the restart Whyte scored an equaliser. Morton regained the lead just before the interval and on the resumption of the second half scored a third to give Hearts an uphill struggle. Noble made the score look a bit more respectable when he scored for the Edinburgh men in the eighty-ninth minute.

The first home game of the season saw Rangers coming through from Glasgow and returning to the west of Scotland with all the points as the result of a 3-1 win. The game was played in dreadful weather as rain fell incessantly throughout the day. What was encouraging, however, was the attendance. Some 8,000 hardy souls, the majority of them Hearts fans, had braved the elements to come to Tynecastle in their continuing and unstinting support and love for their club.

The following week at Broomfield saw six changes to the side which had faced Rangers. Again, the forced chopping and changing of the team resulted in a defeat as Airdrieonians won the encounter 3-2. As it happened, the side lost nine of their first twelve games and by Saturday 28 October the League table showed Hearts occupying third bottom spot, with the two sides beneath them, Motherwell and Raith Rovers, having both played a game less. The bottom of the League did not make for good reading:

	Played	Won	Lost	Drew	For	Against	Points
HEARTS	12	3	9	0	12	28	6
MOTHERWELL	11	2	7	2	17	25	6
RAITH ROVERS	11	0	9	2	6	26	2

It was not as if the side had played badly, although a 6-1 home defeat at the hands of Falkirk on 23 September was a hard one to bear; the problem lay in the forever changing team formation. The week following the mauling by the 'Bairns', Hearts, with another four team changes, went to Celtic Park and gave a full-strength Celtic side a run for their money before going

Peter Nellies. Peter Nellies was born at Kingseat, Dunfermline, in 1885. His father was a collier engineman and because of his work the family moved to the coal mining district of Douglas Water in South Lanarkshire. Peter grew up in that area and on leaving school became a coal miner. He joined the local junior football side, Douglas Water Thistle, and played in the half-back position, now known as the midfield. His performances soon led to recognition in the junior scene and he was capped at junior international level. Heart of Midlothian obtained his signature in April 1908 and he quickly forced himself into the first team and became a fans favourite. Standing at only 5 feet 7 inches and of slight build, he was fearless in the middle of the park. Nellies had other fine attributes necessary to play at a high level; he was a great leader with superb passing and creative skills

and captained the team in the 1914/15 season due to Bob Mercer's extended knee injury. Peter was capped for his country, against Ireland in 1913 and Wales in 1914, and in addition won nine Scottish League international caps. He served the club loyally during the Great War while continuing to work in the Lanarkshire coal mines. Unfortunately his time with Hearts peaked during the war years, which was a lean time for the club, but he played over 450 games and was rewarded with two benefit matches, in 1913 and 1921, against Falkirk and Bradford City respectively. On being released in 1921, Peter joined Kings Park of Stirling and later managed Berwick Rangers. On 12 July 1930 he was involved in a road accident while riding his motor cycle and sustained serious injuries. Three days later, at Glasgow's Royal Infirmary, he died as a result of the injuries.

down 1-0. After the game, the newspapers were full of praise for the spirited performance by the Tynecastle side.

But as is so often the case, in the darkest of times there is always a little bit of sunshine that peeks out from under the clouds and cheers up the Hearts support and way back then was no different: Monday 18 September, Heart of Midlothian 2 Hibernian 1. The gloom lifted, albeit only for a short period, with that victory over their greatest rivals. Amazingly, almost 100 years on, no matter the trials and tribulations, whether it be administration, relegation, a transfer embargo, the economy, redundancies, inflation, petrol going up in price, losing your mobile phone, holiday flight delayed, television breaking down in the middle of a 'live' game, opening up a present on Christmas morning only to find that it's a compact disc of the Proclaimers' Greatest Hits, or the sun shining on Leith, there is nothing that lifts the spirits of the Maroon followers better than a victory over the 'Hibees'.

But still the manager's continual headache over team selections refused to go away. This was due to continuing travel restrictions and military

George Miller. George was born on 21 November 1894 at his parents' home in Dundee Street, Edinburgh. On leaving school he became an apprentice law clerk and eventually became a solicitor with the Coal Commission. He played football for Civil Service Strollers and Tranent Juniors, where he earned three junior international caps. Hearts signed George on 26 September 1915 as an amateur and he quickly settled down at Tynecastle, becoming one of the most creative players with the club at that time. He excelled with his passing skills and close control and was hugely appreciated by the Hearts support, but as for so many others the war interrupted his playing career. He joined the 9th Royal Scots in 1916 and rose to the rank of sergeant, but when on leave would turn out in the maroon jersey. At the end of the war he resumed his career as a solicitor and although Hearts wanted him to sign professional terms, George remained an amateur and concentrated on the field of law. He eventually conceded and signed professional in December 1921 but football hindered his career as a solicitor and he was released in April 1922. In July 1922 Miller joined Raith Rovers and became a star playmaker in one of the Rovers' greatest sides. Raith then introduced a rule that players had to reside in the Kirkcaldy area and this caused work problems for him which saw his return to Hearts in January 1925. George Miller gave Heart of Midlothian tremendous service before being released in April 1931, having played 243 League and Cup games and scored 46 goals. George Miller died on 16 February 1939 at the age of forty-four years after suffering a heart attack.

Norman Findlay. Norman Findlay was born at Walker-upon-Tyne to Scottish parents. He became a shipwright by trade and played football as a goalkeeper with Newcastle City and then Blyth Spartans. Norman signed for Hearts in May 1913 and spent much of his time with Hearts as the reserve goalkeeper. He was one of the first Hearts players to enlist with the 16th Royal Scots. He underwent his military training but as he was a carpenter by trade, Norman's skills were required on the home front and he was not sent to France with the rest of the battalion. Norman was released from military duties in 1916 and began work in the shipyards of Newcastle. After the war he was released by Hearts and joined Coventry City. In later years he moved to Isleworth in Middlesex and worked at repairing barges on the River Thames. Norman Morrison Findlay died in 1949 at Ealing in London, at the age of fifty-nine years.

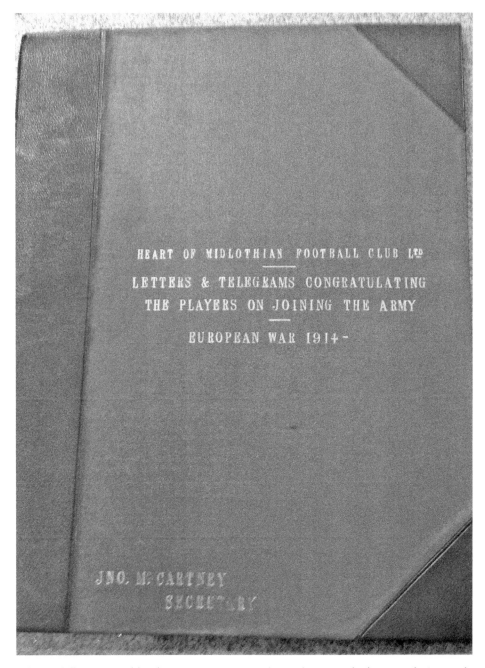

A beautifully presented book containing congratulatory letters and telegrams, from people from all walks of life, to the players on joining the Army in 1914.

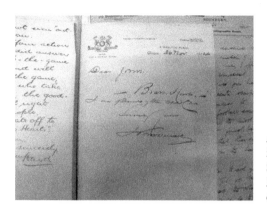

A letter dated 26 November 1914 from John McDowell, President of the Scottish Football Association, to John McCartney. 'Bravo Hearts. I am proud of this old club.'

service demands. McCartney never knew who was available until match day, which was wholly unsatisfactory but he just had to persevere with what was at his disposal. His teams were regularly completed with guest players and players from the junior ranks of Scottish football. Many of the players who were engaged in working in factories or the mines experienced difficulties in getting to the grounds on time from their place of employment. There was no lack of hostile outside sources scrutinising football clubs for infringements of government regulations or even rules of decent conduct.

There was some evidence that, even at the height of the war, not all players took their civilian occupation too seriously. The prodigiously gifted inside forward Patsy Gallagher of Celtic was convicted by a Munitions Tribunal of bad timekeeping and attendance at the engineering factory in Dalmuir where he was employed during the week. As it was a condition of being allowed to play football that all players should have another major occupation, Gallagher was suspended for five weeks and Celtic fined £25 for playing him after his conviction came to their knowledge.

But the problems with playing manpower were worsening all over Scotland. In early December a proposal was made that the duration of a game be cut by ten minutes during December and January to enable players to make it to the ground for the required time. The proposal failed to go through by only one vote, displaying the volume of support for it. Poor wartime train services also added to the problem, especially with the distances required to travel to fulfil a fixture. Ayr United complained bitterly to the Scottish Football League that due to poor train services to and from Aberdeen, an overnight stay was necessitated, adding to an expense they could already ill afford. This was the beginning of a campaign to have the 'Dons' dropped from the League, which would later come to fruition.

The rules relating to players' registration became somewhat relaxed, allowing players to turn out for a club other than their own without being formally transferred. The only requirement was that the club playing the player had the consent in writing of the club with whom the player was registered. From time to time there were some blatant infringements of the rules, resulting in the League Management Committee issuing stern warnings to the clubs involved or sometimes just wagging a prudent finger at them.

But the Hearts support did not complain too much about this. They were well aware of the constraints that were being placed on the management and quite frankly they were just happy to see maroon jerseys on the field and didn't particularly care who filled them.

On 30 December Hearts finished the year with a 1-1 draw against Third Lanark at Cathkin Park, watched by a crowd of 4,000. This was the last game that Harry Graham, Hearts' prolific goalscorer and schemer, would take part in that season. As it happened, he did not return to Tynecastle until 1919. Harry Graham was a qualified dentist and his profession made him exempt from service but he chose to volunteer for the Army and joined the Gloucestershire Regiment. Graham was asthmatic and during his initial training the asthma found him out. He was then transferred to the Royal Army Medical Corps to serve as a dental officer and sent to France. Harry was only in France for a short time before being shipped out to Salonika, now known as Thessaloniki.

LEAGUE TABLE, 30 DECEMBER 1916

	Played	Won	Lost	Drew	For	Against	Points
CELTIC	18	14	0	4	41	7	32
MORTON	20	13	3	4	38	22	30
RANGERS	18	12	3	3	39	12	27
KILMARNOCK	20	11	5	4	35	19	26
AIRDRIEONIANS	20	9	4	7	35	23	25
THIRD LANARK	18	10	3	5	28	17	25
ST MIRREN	20	9	6	5	26	21	23
AYR UNITED	20	9	7	4	26	26	22

PARTICK THISTLE	18	8	6	4	28	14	20
DUMBARTON	20	8	9	3	30	43	19
CLYDE	17	5	3	9	25	22	19
FALKIRK	20	5	8	7	29	29	17
HAMILTON ACADEMICAL	19	5	8	6	21	36	16
HIBERNIAN	21	3	9	9	30	44	15
HEART of MIDLOTHIAN	21	7	13	1	19	36	15
MOTHERWELL	20	5	11	4	31	40	14
QUEEN'S PARK	18	5	10	3	27	37	13
ABERDEEN	20	3	11	6	17	26	12
DUNDEE	20	4	13	3	26	40	11
RAITH ROVERS	20	1	15	4	16	53	6

The new year of 1917 was heralded by a 3-0 defeat in the final of the Wilson Cup by old rivals Hibernian. The game was played at Easter Road before a crowd of 5,500. The next day Hamilton Academical were the vistors and a Hearts side, showing four changes from the day before, won 3-1. But what must have been worrying for the directors of the club about this game was the poor attendance of 2,000. Hearts were now struggling not just on the field but off it as well. It was becoming increasingly difficult for everyone at Tynecastle to keep the club on a firm financial footing.

Then a fully fit Bob Mercer, having recovered from his knee injury, was called into the Armed Services to complete his military training but continued to play when given leave.

The indifferent form of the team continued for the remainder of the season. The only notable highlights were the 'double' over Hibernian and the guest appearances of Chelsea's England international striker George Hilsden. An extremely popular player while with Chelsea and West Ham, his football career was all but ended in 1917 when he suffered from a mustard gas attack at Arras. A weathervane modelled on Hilsdon is still a feature at Stamford Bridge, the home of Chelsea. Legend has it that if the weathervane is removed then the club will suffer misfortune. In the late 1970s the weathervane was removed due to renovations to the stadium and Chelsea experienced footballing and financial problems until it was eventually restored to its rightful place.

Nearing the end of the season, the fabric of the Scottish League was under considerable strain. Clubs who had dropped out of wartime football were expected to continue to pay their subscriptions but no fewer than eight of them, Abercorn, Arthurlie, Clydebank, Dundee Hibernian, East Stirlingshire, Johnstone, Leith Athletic and Vale of Leven, were seriously in arrears. In order to complete the fixture lists, clubs were having to play twice on the same day. Celtic recorded dual victories against Raith Rovers and Motherwell while Clyde played twice against Motherwell and Third Lanark.

The last game of the 1916/17 League campaign was a 1-1 draw with Queen's Park at Hampden on 28 April but not before more bad news had been delivered to the doors of Tynecastle. Information was received that on 22 April another member of the Hearts family had been killed in action in France. This time it was John Allan, who was serving with the 9th Royal Scots. John lost his life at the Battle of Arras in northern France when the Allied troops were mounting an offensive. The battle had begun on 9 April 1917 and lasted until 16 May of that year, by which time almost 160,000 Allied casualties had been reported. Apparently, John had been part of a patrol engaged in reconnoitring a wooded area when he was cut down by enemy crossfire.

Like so many others, John Allan's body was never found. He was thirty years old and had resided at 10 Springwell Place, Edinburgh, with his parents.

John Allan is commemorated on the Arras Memorial at Faubourg d'Amiens Cemetery, Arras. Mercifully, John was the last player that Heart of Midlothian would lose to the Great War.

There was better news when it was learned that Paddy Crossan and Alfie Briggs were making excellent progress in recovering from the wounds they had sustained in France. Both had been taking part in light training sessions at the club, much to the delight of Jimmy Duckorth. Although Alfie had been discharged from the Army by this time, Paddy was still a serving soldier.

The final League table for 1916/17 was as follows:

	Played	Won	Lost	Drew	For	Against	Points
CELTIC	38	27	1	10	79	17	64
MORTON	38	24	8	6	72	39	54
RANGERS	38	24	9	5	68	32	53
AIRDRIEONIANS	38	21	9	8	71	38	50
THIRD LANARK	38	19	8	11	53	37	49

John Allan. Born at Greenlaw, Berwickshire, on 2 March 1887, John moved with his family to Edinburgh at an early age. He attended Dalry Primary School, just a short distance from Tynecastle. Wemyss Athletic was his first club before moving to Tranent Juniors. It was from there that he went to Hearts in October 1914. He was principally a reserve defender who was signed as cover for Bob Mercer. John was regarded as a whole-hearted performer but his only first team outing was against Leith Athletic in the East of Scotland Shield in December 1914. Shortly after the outbreak of war, he enlisted in the 9th Royal Scots. Another who would not pull on the famous maroon jersey again.

Annan Ness. Born in Kirkcaldy in 1892, Annan Ness was initially a miner and at the age of nineteen years he joined the ranks of the Royal Army Medical Corps and served from July 1911 until October 1913. He signed for Hearts in August 1913 from junior side Bonnyrigg Rose Athletic and turned professional in October, after leaving the Army. Annan was one of the players that signed up for McCrae's Battalion on 25 November 1914. As his previous military experience was valued, he quickly rose to the rank of sergeant. He took part in the Somme Offensive on 1 July 1916 and was wounded by shrapnel, which luckily was not considered to be too serious. During the hostilities Sergeant-Major Ness led a number of historic actions and continued to serve his country till the end of the war.

After his return to Tynecastle he cancelled his contract in December 1919 in order to pursue a career as a dentist and later became a qualified dental surgeon.

On 15 December 1942 Annan Buchan Ness passed away in a nursing home in Edinburgh.

KILMARNOCK	38	18	13	7	69	46	43
ST MIRREN	38	15	13	10	49	43	40
MOTHERWELL	38	16	16	6	57	59	38
PARTICK THISTLE	38	14	17	7	44	33	35
DUMBARTON	38	12	15	11	56	73	35
HAMILTON ACADEMICAL	38	13	16	9	53	72	35
FALKIRK	38	12	16	10	58	57	34
CLYDE	38	10	14	14	40	52	34
HEARTS	38	14	20	4	44	59	32
AYR UNITED	38	12	19	7	47	59	31
DUNDEE	38	13	21	4	58	71	30
HIBERNIAN	38	10	18	10	57	72	30
QUEEN'S PARK	38	11	20	7	56	81	29
RAITH ROVERS	38	8	23	7	42	91	23
ABERDEEN	38	7	24	7	36	68	21

One piece of silverware did come Hearts' way when Armadale FC were beaten 5-3 in the Rosebery Charity Cup final at Tynecastle.

These photographs show embroidered silk postcards sent by the author's grandfather from the Western Front to members of the family. The cards were known as 'WW1 Silks' and were first produced in 1914. The cards were hand embroidered on strips of silk mesh and were mostly produced by French and Belgian women refugees who worked in their homes and refugee camps. The finished strips were then forwarded to factories for cutting and mounting on postcards. There was a central portion cut as a flap so that a small printed greeting card with a personal message could be placed inside.

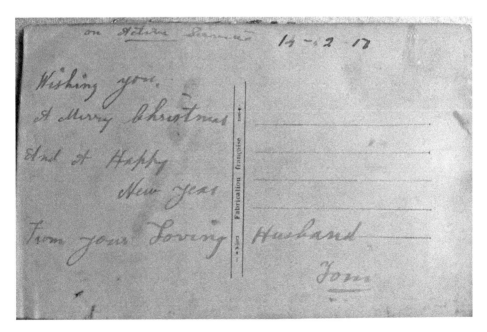

The message on the reverse side reads, 'Wishing you a Merry Christmas and a Happy New Year, from your loving husband Tom' and is dated 14 December 1917.

5

Season 1917/18

The new season began on 18 August and overall attendances throughout the League were reported as being good. There had been changes made to the League formation during the close season. It was clear that matters could not continue as before and in June, Aberdeen and Raith Rovers, the two sides who had finished bottom of the League the previous season, and Dundee were asked to withdraw from the competition due to wartime travel difficulties. Their on-cost charges would be met and to achieve this it was decreed that there would be a 5 per cent deduction from the gate drawings of the clubs continuing in active membership. The three retiring clubs would retain full rights as First Division members, including the right to be represented at meetings of the League. The two Edinburgh sides remained, but the eighteen-club League more or less became a West Central Scotland competition as Clydebank were invited to join in order to even up the numbers. Three other clubs, Albion Rovers, Stevenston United and Vale of Leven, all made application for the vacant spot but Clydebank got the nod. They had enjoyed one season of Second Division membership and their inclusion in the First Division was probably due to the wartime boom in the town among shipyard and munition workers.

A crowd of 6,000 were at Tynecastle, notwithstanding heavy showers of rain, to see Hearts play St Mirren. Making a welcome return to the side were Alfie Briggs and Paddy Crossan, who were given a huge cheer when they ran onto the field of play. The fans were already witnessing a game full of incident when an event took place which would remain a talking point for some time to come. In the second half, with Hearts ahead 2-1, a spectator in the enclosure beneath the Main Stand became abusive towards the 'Buddies' outside right Harry Higginbotham. The St Mirren player took great exception to this tirade of abuse being directed at him and ran over to the boundary fence to confront the miscreant. To the astonishment of everyone within the ground, Higginbotham didn't stop but jumped over the fence and took off in pursuit of the offender along the front of the stand. However, the spectator luckily managed to make good his escape and avoided being caught by the enraged player, much to the merriment of the crowd. Higginbotham's return to the field was short-lived as his indiscretion earned him an early bath. The match referee, G. H. MacKenzie, took a very dim view of Higginbotham's indiscretions and submitted a scathing report to the Scottish Football Association with regards to the incident. The scoreline remained the same, with Hearts being unable to capitalise on their numerical supremacy. But it was a well-deserved victory, with the fans delighted to see the return of two of their favourite sons. A man who was particularly pleased to see them playing again was John McCartney. It was a great occasion for Briggs and Crossan given what they had been through and had witnessed. The last time they had played together in a maroon jersey had been on 4 December 1915, against Aberdeen at Tynecastle, when they were home on leave. But it was an occasion that was also tinged with sadness. Harry Wattie and Duncan Currie had also been in the Hearts' colours that day in what was to prove their final game for the Heart of Midlothian. A lot of water had passed under the bridge since then.

Both Briggs and Crossan retained their places in the side that faced Queen's Park at Hampden the week following. In the 4-0 reversal Paddy had to go off injured when Hearts were two down and didn't return to the action. He would eventually return to pull on the jersey but not until January 1919 and not before he had once again experienced and suffered the ravages of war. Incidentally, two of the 'Spiders' goals in the 4-0 win had come from Alan Morton, who would go on to play for Rangers for many years and thereafter become part of the legendary 'Wembley Wizards' in 1928 when playing for Scotland in the 5-1 defeat of the Auld Enemy.

Following on from the very poor performance against Queen's Park, the support were not looking forward to the visit of Hibernian for the League clash on 1 September. In the first thirty minutes their fears appeared to be well founded as the Easter Road side dominated proceedings. Then, when the Hibs goalkeeper, McManus, saved a penalty from Bert Denyer, the Hearts support became even more apprehensive and agitated. But just before the break they were all smiles when Robert Drummond gave Hearts the lead. Hearts had to weather a fair amount of sustained pressure in the second half but the score remained the same and their fans went home happy. Aye, there's nothing like a derby win to lift the spirits.

But the team's form continued to be erratic and during September, apart from the defeat of Hibernian, a 1-0 home win over Morton was all the support had to cheer. Motherwell and Falkirk both recorded 4-0 home wins over Hearts, with Celtic winning 1-0 at Tynecastle at the end of the month.

The beginning of October saw no improvement, with 4-3 and 4-1 defeats away from home to Kilmarnock and Partick Thistle respectively. It was after the game against Partick that Alfie Briggs decided that he was no longer able to give his best on the field for the club. He had played six matches in his attempted comeback but the wounds he had sustained at the Somme were proving too much even for this brave man. Alfie wrote a letter to the club explaining the reasons for his retirement. The following is an extract from the Hearts Minute Book outlining a letter the directors had received from Briggs: 'Alfred Briggs wrote acknowledging cheque for wages and thanking Directors for kind consideration. He agreed that it was decidedly dangerous for him to play and regretted that he could not give the return his heart desired.'

Very generously, Hearts continued to pay his wages till the end of the season.

In terms of results on the field, November was another disaster with away defeats at Clydebank and Hamilton and home losses to Rangers and Falkirk. The away clash with Clydebank again highlighted massive problems in reaching venues by rail. The train carrying the Hearts party from Edinburgh for the game was late arriving in Glasgow and consequently the start of the game was delayed for thirty minutes. Only forty minutes each way was played against the 'Bankies' to enable Hearts to catch the return train to Edinburgh. The hierarchy of the Scottish League was more than sympathetic towards Hearts, who escaped punishment. Nonetheless, it was decided that the result of the abridged game should stand. But Hearts' financial plight was becoming alarming. The club were now heavily in debt as attendances continued to dwindle, compounded by the fact that most men were working Saturday shifts in factories. The situation reached the embarrassing stage when Hearts were omitted from a war fundraising tournament and due to travel restrictions there were genuine fears that the club would be excluded from the League. But the falling of attendances did not just pertain to Hearts as all the other clubs were experiencing the same problems.

At the end of November, the League placings saw Hearts occupying second-bottom spot.

	Played	Won	Lost	Drew	For	Against	Points
HIBERNIAN	15	3	8	4	20	28	10
CLYDE	14	4	8	2	19	28	10
HEART of MIDLOTHIAN	15	5	10	0	12	23	10
AYR UNITED	15	2	9	4	13	27	8

It was about that time that John McCartney began to notice changes in Jimmy Duckworth, his trusted trainer. 'Duckie' began to have mood swings and appeared to become anxious at the most trivial of things; in essence, he wasn't his normal self. As it happened, Jimmy was at breaking point – completely stressed out. The catastrophic happenings over the previous years were having an adverse effect on his health yet again. It wasn't the first time that McCartney would find Jimmy standing quietly by himself in the empty home dressing room. Jimmy would look round the dressing room and see only spaces where 'his boys' used to sit, engaging in light-hearted and good-natured banter which led to the inevitable fits of laughter. There were many new faces at Tynecastle but the 'boys' were no longer there. Boyd, Currie, Ellis, Gracie, Speedie and Wattie were no longer there. They were gone forever. The dressing room at Tynecastle served only as a reminder to Jimmy of the fate they had met. There was now a void in Jimmy Duckworth's life and it couldn't be filled. The stress and strain was again proving too much for this dedicated and faithful servant of the Heart of Midlothian. At sixty-eight years of age, Jimmy was advised by his GP, Doctor Stevens, to cease working as he had developed a heart problem. Jimmy eventually heeded this advice and took time off work, leaving Tom Murphy in charge.

The remainder of the season continued in the same vein, with the availability of players and transport to and from games still giving John McCartney grief. In fact, McCartney had by now got into the habit of carrying a railway timetable with him at all times. On 12 January 1918, in an away fixture at Ibrox, Hearts were reduced to ten men when one of their players, outside left Fred Gibson, left the field early to go to his place of employment. It will come as no surprise that Rangers won the fixture 2-0. This result left Hearts third bottom of the League with 16 points from

A silk postcard issued by *My Weekly* magazine in 1916. A set of nine cards was produced depicting battles of the First World War, including Loos, Mons, Verdun and Ypres, and they were presented free with the magazine. This one shows the Somme.

THE "MY WEEKLY" BATTLE SERIES.

THE SOMME.

Under Generals Haig and Foch, the Anglo-French forces began a great forward movement on July 1st. The region of the advance was that of the river Somme. The German trenches were first blasted by shell fire and then stormed and captured. Many prisoners were taken and much booty fell into the hands of the Allies.

These beautiful pictures are suitable for decorating Tea Cosies, Table Centres, Chair Backs, and a great variety of similar articles.

They are presented Free in every copy of

"MY WEEKLY."

The Girls' Favourite Paper.

GET IT EVERY WEEK.

Passed for publication by the Press Bureau on September 28th, 1916.

The reverse side gives a brief account of the battle but paints a very rosy and patriotic tale of the event for the reader.

Four of the cards
issued, depicting
Mons, Ypres, the
Marne and Loos.

22 games. But there was a brief revival of their fortunes in respect of results in the early part of 1918, with a fine 3-1 win over their foes Hibernian at Easter Road before a good crowd of some of 10,000 on 2 February. In the early stages of the game Hibs had been by far the better side and the Hearts goalie was a busy man. But after numerous misses, they paid the price when Jimmy Dawson gave Hearts the lead. Two minutes into the second half, George Sinclair doubled Hearts' lead. Willie Miller of Hibernian reduced the leeway with a well-taken goal, but shortly after that Jimmy Dawson restored the two-goal advantage. The bragging rights in the city were still with the Hearts.

Also during the month of February, a quite significant piece of legislation was passed; the Representation of the People Act came into being, allowing women over the age thirty and men of twenty-one years of age the right to vote. Hard on the heels of this, the Ministry of Food announced a new scheme for the rationing of butter, margarine and tea which it was hoped would see an even distribution of these items across the country. Scotland was to be divided into three divisional districts, north, east and west, and households would be issued with ration cards. When obtaining any of the rationed items, these cards were to be presented to the shopkeeper and it became an offence under the Defence of the Realm Act for any shopkeeper to offer inducements or tout for business.

The rationing of good results to the followers of Hearts was also in evidence and in short supply as the indifferent form of their team continued as spring beckoned. Saturday 20 April saw the conclusion of Hearts' League fixtures, which ended with a 3-2 defeat by St Mirren at Love Street, Paisley, with this formation: Black; Garrett, Kiernan; McIntosh, Lochhead, Ross; Honeyman, Nellies, Sharp, Barnes, Gibson.

The season's end saw Hearts ending up mid-table with 32 points from 34 games, with Rangers lifting the League title having amassed 56 points. Quite frankly, it was a season that everyone at Tynecastle was just glad to see the back of. Of the 34 League games played, they had won only 14, with 16 losses and 4 draws.

The final League table for 1917/18 was as follows:

	Played	Won	Lost	Drew	For	Against	Points
RANGERS	34	25	3	6	66	24	56
CELTIC	34	23	3	7	66	26	55
KILMARNOCK	34	19	10	5	69	41	43

MORTON	34	17	8	9	53	42	43
MOTHERWELL	34	16	9	9	70	51	41
PARTICK THISTLE	34	14	8	12	51	37	40
DUMBARTON	34	13	13	8	48	49	34
QUEEN'S PARK	34	14	14	6	64	63	34
CLYDEBANK	34	14	5	5	55	56	33
HEART of MIDLOTHIAN	34	14	6	4	41	58	32
ST MIRREN	34	11	16	7	42	50	29
HAMILTON ACADEMICAL	34	11	17	6	52	63	28
THIRD LANARK	34	10	17	7	56	62	27
FALKIRK	34	9	16	9	38	58	27
AIRDRIEONIANS	34	10	18	6	46	58	26
HIBERNIAN	34	18	17	9	42	57	25
CLYDE	34	9	23	2	37	72	20
AYR UNITED	34	5	20	9	32	61	19

The following is part of a report by the club's directors at the end of the 1917/18 season taken from the Minute Book and describes perfectly Hearts' fortunes at that period in history:

> The Directors herewith submit the PROFIT and LOSS ACCOUNT and BALANCE SHEET of the COMPANY as at 30th April, 1918, which shows a loss on the year's workings of £189, 14s 2d after allowing for depreciation.
>
> The Credit Balance now stands at £3174, 0s. 5d.
>
> The Cash Funds at the date of the close of the Accounts amount to £244, 10s. 4d.
>
> The Directors wish to place on record their appreciation of the efforts of the players as a whole and also their indebtedness to Soldier Players for their valuable assistance among who may be mentioned:
>
> Sergt. John McIntosh (Hull City), Highland Light Infantry.
>
> Private Andrew Wilson (Middlesboro'), Royal Scots.
>
> C.S.M. Matthew Lochhead (Swindon), Royal Scots Fusiliers.
>
> The carrying-on of the game during the past season has taxed more than ever the energies of the Club Officials in general, and it is pleasing in this connection to record that supporters fully recognised

the difficulties and uncertainties which attended the placing of teams on the field from week to week.

Having regard to the ever-increasing calls of our Country for men and munitions, and also the further restrictions foreshadowed on railway travelling, it is futile to attempt, at the moment, any forecast as to the immediate future of football.

Nevertheless, the gratifying measure of support accorded during the past three seasons has justified the continuance of the game, and warrants every endeavour being made to carry it into another season – granted possible conditions. This for the sake of supporters at home. What of those engaged elsewhere? The injunction, repeated in letters from all parts of our far-flung battle line:- 'Keep on doing, we shall soon be back' – may surely be taken as evidence that the continuance of the game appeals to them as a cheering indication of the height of the homeland barometer.

E. H. FURST
Chairman.
JNO. McCartney, Secretary
Tynecastle Park, Gorgie Road,
Edinburgh, 29 May, 1918

Crossan, having been declared fit again for active duty, had been posted to the Middle East with the 4th Royal Scots. The wage book, which can still be viewed at Tynecastle, bears the inscription 'Gone to Egypt'. His regiment joined up with the Egyptian Expeditionary Force, which was engaged in the Sinai and Palestine Campaign. This was the Middle Eastern theatre of the war and was being fought between soldiers of the British Empire and the Ottoman Empire, who were being supported by the Germans. Fighting had broken out in January 1915 when German-led Ottoman troops invaded the Sinai Peninsula, then part of the British Protectorate of Egypt. The fighting going on there was generally not well known or indeed properly understood, with public opinion being that the resources would be better deployed on the Western Front. Nonetheless, vitally important battles had taken place, namely the Battle of Mughaar Bridge fought between 12 and 14 November 1917 and the Battle of Jerusalem which had taken place between 12 November and 30 December 1917. Paddy Crossan fought at the Battle of Jerusalem.

In the spring of 1918 the Germans mounted a series of attacks along the Western Front. It became known as the Spring Offensive or the Ludendorff Offensive and began on 21 March 1918. It was viewed as the Germans' 'last throw of the dice' and they threw virtually everything they had at the Allies. The general plan was to break through the Allied lines and outflank the British forces which held the front from the Somme River to the English Channel, bringing about the defeat of the British Army. The fighting was ferocious, with the loss of thousands of lives on both sides. Due to the serious losses the British had to send reinforcements from the Egyptian Expeditionary Force to the Western Front. In April Paddy Crossan was transferred back to France from the Middle East.

After the initial attacks the German advance began to falter and in August 1918 the Allies began a counter-offensive which eventually led to the capitulation of the German Empire. Again, it came at a price and casualties were heavy. New weapons brought new ways to inflict death, injuries and suffering and the introduction of what became known as chemical warfare was no exception. The Germans had been using poison gas to fight the war and Crossan was severely gassed during the hostilities at Hendecourt-les-Cagnicourt, south-east of Arras. Fortunately, Paddy survived the gassing and thankfully was sent home once more to recuperate. How ironic war can be; Crossan had been injured at the Battle of the Somme by the enemy and a German prisoner of war had saved his limb from amputation. Some months before the war ended, the enemy had made yet another unsuccessful attempt on his life. The man described as 'the handsomest man in Scottish football' was now without question 'the luckiest man in Scottish football'.

By coincidence Bob Mercer, who was serving at the Somme at that time with the Royal Garrison Artillery, was also badly gassed during an attack. Bob was eventually shipped back home but the injury by gassing he suffered would have catastrophic effects on his health in years to come. More bad news arrived when it was learned that Neil Moreland, who had been fighting since the outbreak of the war, had once again been wounded in France. Was there to be no end to this killing and wounding and wrecking of young lives? Mercifully, there was soon to be light at the end of this extremely dark and long tunnel.

In the summer of 1918 the Scottish Football League found themselves in a bit of a quandary. The German war effort was disintegrating rapidly and it was beginning to look as if hostilities would come to an end sooner rather than later, but not before the season was due to begin in August.

War conditions still prevailed and difficulties with transport were still to the fore, as was the shortage of players with conscription biting savagely. These factors lay behind the proposal, which was approved in July, that Ayr

United and Falkirk be omitted from the League for the 1918/19 season. As expected, this brought about a furious response from both clubs and their supporters. To this end, a meeting in Ayr attracted an audience of 800 and, in a calculated swipe at Celtic and Rangers, it was maintained that it would be preposterous to exclude the Ayrshire side from the League, a club whose contribution to the armed services in manpower was only exceeded by that of Hearts and Queen's Park. The League management committee had a major rethink and allowed both clubs to continue in active membership. There was no doubt that, if the decision was taken for reasons of transport problems, there were no logical grounds for allowing clubs from the west of Scotland to pass a boarded up Brockville Park, Falkirk, while en route by train to play games at Easter Road or Tynecastle, some 20 miles further east. It had even been mooted in some circles that both Edinburgh clubs would be excluded from the League set-up because of the travelling difficulties being experienced by teams from the west. But weren't Hearts and Hibernian facing the same problems when travelling from the east of Scotland? It was probably at this point that someone from the Scottish League management asked the question, 'Are we missing something here?' Thankfully common sense, which was occasionally in short supply, was applied and the League formation remained the same.

6

Season 1918/19

The emergency provisions regarding unregistered players were being blatantly abused on all sides as everyone adopted a cavalier approach to the rules. In an effort to regularise the situation, it was decreed by the League that no club could play the same player under emergency provision no more than twice in any one month and thereafter one full month had to elapse before the said player was eligible to play again; and so the season began with these words of warning ringing in the ears of the clubs.

In keeping with the availability of players, it was yet again a very much-changed Hearts side that took to the field at Cappielow to face Morton on the opening game of the season on 17 August. The following eleven went down 2-0 to the Greenock men: Black; Lochhead, Kiernan; Sharp, Brown, Ross; Sinclair, McKay, Ambler, Dawson, Neave.

It was a disappointing start and that theme continued until 21 September, when they recorded their first victory – a 2-1 win over Dumbarton at Boghead.

But the game still wasn't without humour. The Dumbarton player Felix Gunn was arrested for failing to return the certificate exempting him from military service because he was a miner – he had been unemployed for a number of months and nowhere near the coal mines. In their defence Dumbarton said that they had no knowledge of this and were surprised as 'Gunn's appearance was always neat and tidy'. As Gunn would have had to come to the football ground straight from his work at the coal mine on numerous occasions, the explanation wasn't fully accepted by the authorities.

The public had a wee laugh to themselves when the story first appeared in print but the laughter quickly ceased when a flu pandemic, which had been affecting numerous countries worldwide, causing millions of deaths, hit the shores of Scotland. Initially there had been reported outbreaks of the virus in the west of Scotland in April 1918. It was thought that soldiers returning from France had carried the flu virus back to Scotland with them. Whatever the theory, the virus quickly spread and by October the disease had become more virulent, with over 300 people dying every week in Glasgow alone. An added problem in towns and cities throughout Scotland was that many doctors were still serving overseas, causing a chronic shortage of medical cover and resources. It was understood that the disease was being spread by infected people coming into contact with others and in view of this it was recommended that sufferers remained at home. Many schools were closed and the public were discouraged from going to the cinemas or theatres and any such places, including football grounds, where many people gathered. The flu struck in mostly densely populated towns and cities and Edinburgh and Leith were among the areas affected. It struck young and old alike and due to the rationing and absence of nutritional foods, bodies which were undernourished were particularly susceptible to the disease. It wasn't until well after the war had finished that it was brought under control, by which time thousands had died in this country and millions throughout the globe.

But the end of the Great War was now in sight. Germany was on its knees. Already the sailors of the High Seas Fleet at Kiel and Wilhelmshaven had mutinied on 29 October, after being ordered to carry out a last, futile mission against the Allies. Economic disaster and social disorder was now spreading across Germany. Having exhausted its resources on the battlefields, it now sought an armistice with the Allies in the early part of November 1918. On 7 November German delegates arrived in Compiegne, France, to negotiate the terms of the armistice. The armistice was duly signed in Marshal Foch's railway carriage in the Forest of Compiegne at 0510 hours on the morning of 11 November.

The commander-in-chief of all Allied forces on the Western Front, Ferdinand Foch, then sent a telegram message to all his commanders, informing them that hostilities would finally come to an end at 1100 hours that morning; and so at the eleventh hour of the eleventh day of the eleventh month of 1918, the Great War came to an end. The Western Front fell silent as the guns that had thundered for four years stopped firing. It was over and the lamps in Europe were relit.

All over the world people in villages, towns and cities rejoiced and the church bells rang out. The people began to celebrate and Scotland was no exception. Men, women and children were dancing in the streets, many singing the National Anthem as the news began to sink in.

In Scotland's capital city, the scenes of joy were unrestrained. The scenes were being repeated in the streets of Glasgow. In the Lanarkshire town of Hamilton, the regimental brass band and pipers of the Scottish Rifles paraded through the streets, playing patriotic tunes. Just a few miles up the road in Motherwell, nurses and soldiers marched through the industrial town to the sound of music from the Motherwell Boys' Brigade bugle band. The residents of Musselburgh were treated to the sight of aeroplanes flying over the town, dropping light signals. The good people of Dundee greeted the news with the sounds of factory hooters and fog horns from the boats and ships out on the Tay. The Granite City, the home of the Gordon Highlanders, celebrated in style with public and private buildings a mass of bunting and Union flags. The celebrations in Aberdeen reached their peak when a huge procession headed by the Gordon Highlanders, with bands playing and flags flying, marched through the main streets of the famous old city. The festivities lasted well into the wee sma' oors.

Back in Edinburgh, the good folk of the city were now retiring for the evening but still flushed with the excitement of the war having come to an end. The capital was quietening down and lights began to go out in the households as a happy and untroubled sleep took over.

Out to the west of the city in Gorgie, a famous landmark sat quietly in the darkness. The front doors of Tynecastle Park were closed and locked for the night. The only sounds to be heard coming from within the Main Stand was Blackie the cat, carrying out his nightly patrol in the search of mice. But wait … was that the faint sound of voices and laughter coming from the home dressing room? Blackie stopped and listened with his ears pricked up. The voices sounded familiar to him. Were the voices he heard that of James Speedie, Tom Gracie, Duncan Currie, Ernie Ellis, Harry Wattie, Jimmy Boyd and John Allan, all of whom he knew so well but hadn't seen for a while? Had they come 'home' again?

Blackie continued to listen intently outside the door but heard nothing more. 'Och,' he thought to himself, 'Ah'm getting auld an' startin' tae hear things that are no' there,' as he wandered off to resume his patrol duties. We can only imagine that Blackie was indeed hearing things … but maybe, just maybe, Speedie, Gracie, Currie, Ellis, Wattie, Boyd and Allan had all returned home to Tynecastle – a place where they will always be remembered. They will always be there.

Many years later, Willie Montgomery, who had been a member of the ground staff at the club since 1954, confided in David Speed, the club's historian, that he had often heard unusual noises in the Main Stand when he was working late at night. Initially, Willie had attributed it to the wooden and metal construction simply contracting or expanding, but the noises continued and Willie became convinced that the strange sounds he had heard were not that easily explained away. Even now, some members of staff engaged in duties during the hours of darkness have also spoken about the strange goings on in the deserted stand and they, as Willie Montgomery was, are not totally convinced that it is structural movement. Of course, the logical explanation is that the noises heard are indeed from the structures. Or are they?

It was no coincidence that Hearts' next game at Tynecastle on Saturday 16 November turned out to be their best performance of the season as they beat Third Lanark 5-0. Before the game there was a different feel to the atmosphere as the fans made their way to the ground. After so many years of uncertainty, the crowd had a certain spring to their step and were in a carefree and buoyant mood. The 7,000 people within Tynecastle that afternoon were in good voice as the Grassmarket Band led them in the singing of patriotic songs. They had every reason to be in good voice.

There was a special welcome back to Tynecastle for some brave individuals. A Main Stand season ticket was given to returning members of the 16th Royal Scots C Company who had been Hearts season ticket holders, shareholders, officials or indeed players. At the start of the hostilities, the club had made a promise to these men that they would be given this on their return from the war. On the reverse of the ticket was printed the crest of the Royal Scots, and inside was the person's, name, rank and service number. The following statement was also included: 'Voluntarily these men went forth to fight for King and Country. The gloomiest hour in the nation's history found them ready. As pioneers in the formation of a brilliant regiment, sportsman the world over will ever remember them. Duty well done, they are welcomed back to Tynecastle; Hearts of Oak.'

Around eighty special passes were issued; Heart of Midlothian just wished it had been more.

As the servicemen and women began to return home, ordinary season ticket sales increased to 850. For many of those returning, it was their first view of the impressive Main Stand, and overall the ground was in admirable condition, with the banking and wooden terraces having been refilled with

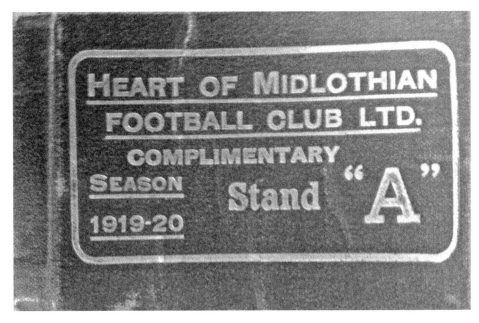

The season ticket issued for the Main Stand.

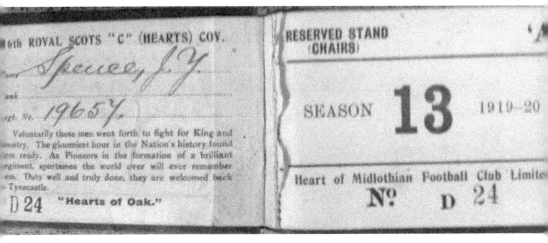

The inside of the book.

The rear cover, showing the crest of the Royal Scots.

fresh ash. The players also looked the part, with £85 being paid out for new football kit.

The end of the war meant that the remainder of the season was played in a peculiar half-world as the nation adjusted and tried to return to normality. But the signing of the Armistice and peace in France did not bring goodwill in the footballing circles of Scotland as referee James Sinclair, who had been in charge of a match at Airdrieonians' Broomfield, could testify. Bristling with anger and indignation, he penned the following to the Management Committee.

Dear Sir,
I must take exception and report Manager Chapman of Airdrieonians for using language to me (before the Balcony Seat holders) when I

was entering my dressing room. He seemed to feel against a decision which was not awarded (*sic*). He made a remark 'Ah, you twister! Was it going to burst your coupon if Airdrie won?' Immediately the spectators from the Balcony heard his remarks, they too had language to use which I am sure could and should have been left unsaid. I may add that instead of some of the Officials being there as protection against such conduct, I am sorry to say that they started a scene which I trust I will not figure in again.

Yours truly,

Jas. S. Sinclair.

When questioned, Mr Chapman admitted to the contents of the letter but claimed that he had done so in a light-hearted manner and no offence was intended. The Management Committee, somewhat unconvinced and unimpressed by this response, fined him four guineas (£4 4s) for his troubles.

As the Hearts players started to return from the war, it was anticipated that the team would begin to show consistency, something which had been absent for some time. But it wasn't as simple as that. It would take a bit of time before these men regained full fitness, both mentally and physically, and there were varying degrees of health and fitness. For some of them, the horrors they had witnessed and the mental scars would stay with them till their dying days. They were not supermen and did not belong to a special generation. They were just ordinary men from ordinary homes who had fought to save their country.

With the war being over, players with all First League clubs were of the view that the wage structure they had enjoyed before wartime conditions were introduced should be reinstated. A meeting of all the captains or deputies of the clubs was called in Glasgow on 14 December 1918 to discuss the players' position regarding the question of wages. It was agreed that the Scottish League be approached to lift the restriction on salaries which had been in force for the previous four years and return to pre-war conditions, with 1 January 1919 being the starting point for the new conditions. It was felt by the players that they had loyally stood by their clubs during the war years in order to keep the game going for the benefit of the public, despite adverse conditions and low wages, and that their demands could not be termed as extortionate. At the conclusion of the meeting a letter was dispatched to the offices of the Scottish Football League informing them of the meeting and outlining the players' views.

The League's response was swift and to the point – No. They felt that the proposed date of 1 January 1919 was too soon to revert to pre-war conditions. The present wage of £1 per week would continue but clubs in profit could apply to pay an extra pound up to 31 December 1918 and £3 per week thereafter. A meeting was then arranged between the two bodies but the League would not move from the decision taken and it was a discontented group of players' representatives who returned to their respective clubs to break the news to their colleagues.

On 11 January 1919 there was cause for good cheer out Gorgie way when it was announced that Paddy Crossan would make his long-awaited comeback for Hearts in the game against bottom-of-the-League Hibernian that afternoon.

Again, we can only imagine how Crossan felt as he took to the field that cold winter's day. He had quite literally been to hell and back and here he was returning to his old stamping ground again, something I'm sure even he could not have envisaged given his experiences.

The game itself was over as a contest before half time. An Andy Wilson hat trick saw to that, his goals coming in the third, sixth and thirty-fifth minute of the game. Hibs did pull a goal back in the second half but it was only a token gesture and Hearts were worthy 3-1 winners.

Meanwhile, it was announced that, to mark the end of the fighting, clubs would compete for the Victory Cup. The Scottish Cup competition was still suspended. It was agreed that the eighteen League clubs along with eight clubs from the Western League would be entered. The Western League was an organisation which had given refuge to some pre-war Second Division clubs and the teams who entered from that league were Abercorn, Albion Rovers, Vale of Leven, Johnstone, Dumbarton Harp, Stevenston United, Renton and Arthurlie. The Victory Cup competition began in March and Hearts were afforded a bye in the first round. With the exception of Albion Rovers, all the clubs from the Western league were eliminated in the first-round ties. Hearts were then drawn away to Third Lanark in the next round, an obstacle they successfully overcame by two goals to one but for which they were made to fight all the way. Andy Wilson gave Hearts a first-half lead but Third Lanark equalised in the second half through a penalty scored by their left-back Robert Orr. Hearts were then awarded a spot kick in the closing stages of the game, which Andy Wilson converted. But the win had come at a cost, with the popular Paddy Crossan, who had turned in an excellent performance, being injured near the end.

The third round, the quarter-finals, saw them back in Glasgow, this time to play Partick Thistle at Firhill without the services of the injured Crossan. It was a competition that was proving very popular with the public. Before a quite amazing attendance of 35,000, Hearts triumphed 2-0 with both goals, which came in the latter stages of the game, again being scored by Andy Wilson. Andy was a player with Middlesbrough who had been invalided from the Army due to a serious injury to his left arm. Hearts had managed to secure his services and what a signing he turned out to be, scoring on a regular basis for them.

In the other ties, Rangers had gone down 1-0 to Airdrieonians, Hibernian defeated Motherwell 2-0 and, perhaps in the surprise of the day, St Mirren had beaten favourites Celtic 1-0 at Love Street after extra-time. Celtic's legendary Patsy Gallagher had even contrived to miss a spot kick in the extra period.

In the semi finals, due to be played on 19 April, Hearts were drawn at home to Airdrieonians while city neighbours Hibernian took on St Mirren at Easter Road.

In a devastating display of football, the Lanarkshire side were simply taken apart by Hearts, with Andy Wilson again being the darling of the support. Wilson hit the net four times in the 7-1 rout before what was then the largest crowd, 44,500, to watch a football match outside of Glasgow. For their efforts in reaching the final, the players were rewarded with a £10 bonus. The net gate receipts from the game were £985, with the government taking £411 in tax.

Andy Wilson.

But any hopes of a Hearts *v*. Hibernian final were dashed when the 'Buddies' ran out 3-1 winners over the Easter Road men. Despite being a goal down at the interval, the Paisley side equalised through Jamie Thomson to take the tie to extra time. Hibs were unfortunate to lose the services of their prolific goalscorer Bobby Gilmour when he left the field with a broken collarbone and thereafter the ten men struggled for the remainder of the game. Another goal by Thomson and one from John Clark saw St Mirren safely into the final to face Hearts.

The much-awaited Victory Cup final took place in Glasgow at Celtic Park on 26 April, with 60,000 there to see what turned out to be an absorbing match. Outwith the 'Saints' fans, this was a game that probably the whole of Scotland wanted Hearts to win due to the sacrifices they had made during the war years. There is no doubt that Hearts would have been popular winners, but it was not to be.

The teams lined up:

Hearts: W. Black; R. Birrell, J. Wilson; R. Preston, R. Mercer, J. Sharp; G. Sinclair, G. Miller, A. Wilson, A. McCulloch, W. Wilson.

St Mirren: W. O'Hagan; J. Marshall, J. Fulton; R. Perry, H. McKenna, H. Anderson; F. Hodges, T. Page, J. Clark, C. Sutherland, J. Thomson.

In the first half, especially the first thirty minutes, Hearts were totally in command and dominated proceedings but just couldn't find the net. Time after time, their quite excellent play broke down at the crucial point.

The second half went much the same way but still the score remained blank as Hearts struggled to break down a very well-organised Saints rearguard. The game then went to extra time but it was now St Mirren in the ascendency as Hearts began to tire. Charlie Sutherland gave them the lead and two minutes later Frank Hodges doubled their score. There was no way back for the brave Hearts and a broken side conceded a third goal near the end.

The Victory Cup was still in the making and the victorious St Mirren team were presented with a shield. When the cup was finally finished, it was presented to the club and both trophies are displayed in the St Mirren boardroom at New Love Street.

Not taking anything away from St Mirren, who were deserving winners, but how pleasing and satisfying it would have been if the Victory Cup had been won by Hearts and the trophies resided in the boardroom at Tynecastle to be a lasting and fitting tribute to the men who had served their country for a shilling a day.

As it happened, Hearts' final League game of the 1918/19 season was away to St Mirren on 10 May. Honours were divided in the 3-3 draw.

It was pleasing to note that the average home gate in the League had increased to 9,412.

The final League placings were as follows:

	Played	Won	Lost	Drew	For	Against	Points
CELTIC	34	26	2	6	71	22	58
RANGERS	34	26	3	5	85	16	57
MORTON	34	18	5	11	76	38	47
PARTICK THISTLE	34	17	10	7	62	43	41
AYR UNITED	34	15	11	8	62	53	38
MOTHERWELL	34	14	10	10	51	41	38
HEART of MIDLOTHIAN	34	14	11	9	59	52	37
QUEEN'S PARK	34	15	14	5	59	57	35
KILMARNOCK	34	14	13	7	61	59	35
CLYDEBANK	34	12	14	8	52	65	32
ST MIRREN	34	10	12	12	43	55	32
THIRD LANARK	34	11	14	9	60	62	31
AIRDRIEONIANS	34	9	14	11	45	54	29
HAMILTON ACADEMICAL	34	11	18	5	49	75	27
DUMBARTON	34	7	19	8	32	58	22
CLYDE	34	7	21	6	45	75	20
FALKIRK	34	6	20	8	46	73	20
HIBERNIAN	34	5	26	3	30	91	13

The body of the Unknown Warrior crossing the Channel aboard the destroyer HMS *Verdun*. The interment of the Unknown Warrior at Westminster Abbey in 1922 would provide relief for many families of soldiers whose remains could not be identified. (J&C McCutcheon Collection)

7

1919 and Beyond

With attendances increasing, this generated solid income for Hearts and, with the profit made from the run in the Victory Cup competition, the club had the satisfaction of making the final payments due on the Main Stand. The chairman and his directors were worthy of the praise they received for this achievement. But the rebuilding of the team had to start from almost scratch. It would take years and would be a slow and sometimes painful process. In October 1919, John McCartney left Heart of Midlothian.

By this time Jimmy Duckworth was seventy years of age and in May 1920 the directors decided that they wanted a younger man to be trainer. Jimmy fully understood their thinking and he agreed to work alongside the new man in an advisory capacity and this suited all parties. The new trainer was to be Charles Dunning, and Jimmy was looking forward to helping out in the coming season. Tragically, 'Duckie' never had the opportunity to fulfil his role. His health began to fail very quickly and he passed away on 25 August 1920. Jimmy Duckworth was buried at Cathcart Cemetery in Glasgow. Heart of Midlothian had lost a valued servant and a great friend who was always there when needed.

On 22 May 1920 Hearts played Celtic at Tynecastle for the benefit of the Scottish National War Memorial Fund. Before a crowd of 15,000, the Glasgow side won 2-0 in a highly entertaining game. For their efforts, both teams were presented with gold medals to mark the occasion.

It was at that time, in response to the request of the shareholders and the public, that the directors undertook the erection of a memorial to the players and members of the club who had given up their lives in the war. Thereafter, negotiations began with Edinburgh Corporation regarding the club's own war memorial, which was originally planned for the major junction at the foot of Ardmillan.

An action shot from the game looking from the Gorgie end of the ground.

Hearts and Celtic
players photographed
together at Tynecastle
on 22 May 1920 for
the fundraising game.

The gold medal presented to the players, marking the occasion. This one was presented to Bob Mercer.

The reverse side of the medal, showing the inscription.

The tablet bearing the names of the Heart of Midlothian directors
instrumental in the building of the new stand.

In September 1921 the tablet giving the names of the directors who were
involved in the building of the Main Stand was finally completed in bronze
at a cost of £30 by Messrs. W. Black & Sons and as unveiled at Tynecastle.

Also in September, a crowd of 5,000 watched an Edinburgh Select play
a Glasgow Select at Tynecastle in a fundraising game for the Heart of
Midlothian War Memorial.

In January 1922 a major change took place when the club learned that
the Tramway Company wanted to run rails through the intended site at
Ardmillan. Edinburgh Corporation apologised for the late change but
offered an alternative site at what was then the horses' fountain in front
of Haymarket Station. This was a popular choice, as besides being one
of the most important street junctions in Edinburgh, the Haymarket was
the gateway, as it were, to the district with which the Heart of Midlothian
Football Club had been for so many years associated.

On Sunday 9 April 1922, the memorial to the Heart of Midlothian
players and members who fell in the Great War was unveiled by the
Secretary of State for Scotland, The Right Honourable Robert Munro
KC, MP, before a crowd of some 35,000. John McCartney was among

The unveiling ceremony at the Haymarket on 9 April 1922.

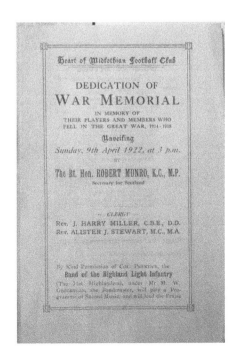

The Order of Service for the ceremony.

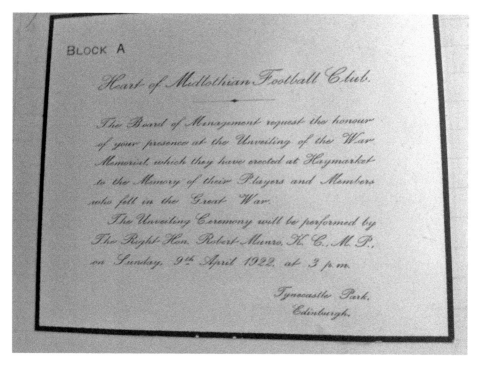

An invitation to attend the ceremony.

The War Memorial looking from the east.

This photograph was taken on Remembrance Sunday, 1948. Note the police officers wearing helmets.

A view taken in the early 1960s, with the police officers now wearing the modern flat cap.

the invited guests. It was an impressive ceremony, with Robert Munro delivering an unforgettable speech. The massive crowd heard the following from him: 'Hearts had shown on the battlefield that courage, resource, skill, endurance, dash and daring that made them famous on the football field. Thank God for men like the Hearts players who fell in the morning of their days and saved the British people from destruction.'

At a reunion dinner of the 16th Battalion Royal Scots on 25 April 1919, held in the North British Hotel, Edinburgh, it was suggested that cairns be erected in Edinburgh and at the Somme in memory of the men who had fallen. Due to lack of funding and the cost, which made the project unfeasible, the plans were abandoned. However, the subject would be broached at other reunion dinners over the years, but the cost always remained an issue. They still felt strongly about the cairn in France and thought it was wrong that their comrades hadn't been remembered as they wished. As they got older, their wish to have 'a wrong righted' grew faint.

It was obvious that the public wished to move on from the time of the Great War. Too much suffering and grief had been brought to too many homes and the country wanted to put it behind them. This was evident when a book written by William Reid, entitled *The Story of the Hearts, 1874–1924*, a fifty-year retrospective, was published in 1924. Only a few pages of the book were dedicated to the war, with the author stating: 'Over the war one is not tempted to linger.' With the passage of time, the building of a cairn in France was largely forgotten.

In 2003, while employed as Safety and Security Manager at Tynecastle, the author was approached by Hearts supporter Jim Paris, who expressed concern that there was no memorial on the Western Front to commemorate the club's players who had died in the Great War. As a result of this meeting, the Hearts Great War Memorial Committee was formed to address the issue. Jim Paris and the author were joined by Robin Beath, then chairman of the Federation of Hearts Supporters Clubs, and by Hearts historian David Speed. They remained uncertain about what form the memorial should take until Jim Paris mentioned that military historian Jack Alexander (who lived in Edinburgh) was on the point of publishing a definitive account of the history of the 16th Royal Scots. Mr Alexander was invited to Tynecastle to address the group and he explained the story of the commemorative cairn that was never built. Jack had taken up the struggle on behalf of the battalion survivors but (like them) had received several rebuffs to his cairn proposal over the

A programme for the reunion dinner of
the 16th Battalion, The Royal Scots, 25
April 1919.

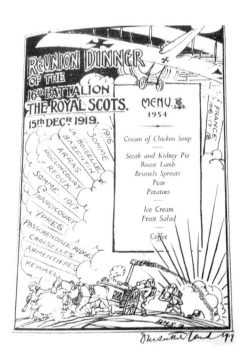

A programme for the 1954 reunion
dinner.

The guests and members of the Hearts Great War Memorial Committee who attended the first fundraising dinner at Tynecastle, Remembrance Sunday, 2003. From left to right, back row: Scott Wilson, Craig Levein, Rod Petrie, Jim Paris, Alan Owenson, Robin Beath, Chris Robinson and David Speed. Front row: Major-General Mark Strudwick, Jack Alexander, Tom Purdie, Bob Crampsey, John Gahagan and Willie Lyle.

years. It was decided unanimously to ask him to join the committee and thereafter Alan Owenson was brought on board to act as official secretary of the fundraising campaign. The purpose of the group was to raise sufficient funds to erect the cairn in the village of Contalmaison on the Somme that had been proposed all those years ago and largely forgotten about.

Fundraising dinners, with guest speakers, were organised with the first one taking place on Remembrance Day 2003 within the Gorgie Suite at Tynecastle. Among the notable guests were Major-General Mark Strudwick, Colonel of the Royal Scots, Hibernian's chairman Rod Petrie, and Scottish football historian Bob Crampsey, with Chris Robinson and Craig Levein representing Heart of Midlothian.

Thereafter, other dinners were held in Prestonpans in East Lothian, Bathgate in West Lothian and Kirkcaldy in the Kingdom of Fife. All these events attracted huge numbers and the tickets sold out very quickly.

Appeals were also made through various Scottish newspapers, leading to people from far and wide making generous individual donations. Heart of Midlothian kindly gave permission for a bucket collection to be made at Tynecastle when Hearts entertained Rangers at Tynecastle. The response of the Ibrox supporters was tremendous. The fans of Hearts and Rangers contributed generously and without question, along with many descendents of the battalion who Jack Alexander had contacted during the course of his extensive researches. The overall response from the public was amazing and the sum of £65,000, which included donations from the Scottish Executive, Edinburgh Council, the Willie Bauld Club, Hearts FC and also the 16th Royal Scots Regiment, was raised.

The unique 'poppy strip' worn in the fixture against Aberdeen on Sunday 9 November 2003.

Perhaps the spirit of the fundraising is summed up perfectly by this particular story: one Thursday morning, pension day in Gorgie, an old lady came into the reception area at Tynecastle and handed over a £5 note to the receptionist on duty. 'That's for the fund,' were all the words that were spoken by her, and with that she was gone. It came with no name, address or fuss but the money was obviously part of her pension which she had uplifted that day from the post office in Gorgie Road. It was a touching gesture, typical of so many who donated from across the UK. Once more, the Hearts support had excelled.

In November 2003, a 'poppy strip' was produced for the first time by Hearts to be worn for the away Scottish Premier League fixture against Aberdeen on 9 November, Remembrance Day. The fixture had been originally scheduled for Saturday 8 November, but as Hearts had been in France mid-week, playing Bordeaux in the UEFA cup, the game was to be played the following day. The kick-off at Pittodrie had been put back an hour to allow the Hearts players and management to attend the annual ceremony at the Haymarket before travelling north.

In the away dressing room at Pittodrie, the Hearts manager Craig Levein gave a last-minute team talk to the players before they took to the field. Pointing at the poppy which adorned the strip, he simply said, 'This game is for them.' Hearts won the difficult fixture 1-0.

In the interim, permission was granted by the French authorities for the construction of the cairn to go ahead after sterling work carried out behind the scenes by Bernard Senechal, the Mayor of Contalmaison, Julian Hutchings, President of Alliance France-Ecosse and Jack Alexander.

The handsome cairn, made of Elgin sandstone and Caithness slate, was built in less than a year and was unveiled on 7 November 2004. The unveiling was performed by Sir George McCrae's grandsons, George McCrae and Ken Hall. Major-General Mark Strudwick, Colonel of the Royal Scots, gave the main address.

It was a fitting tribute. The wishes of the men from the Great War had at long last been realised and a wrong had been righted.

The following morning *The Scotsman* carried the following report of the ceremony:

A commemorative stone cairn has been unveiled in France in memory of Scots soldiers who fought in the 1916 Battle of the Somme. The memorial honours the men of the 16th Royal Scots, including the

The cairn at Contalmaison.

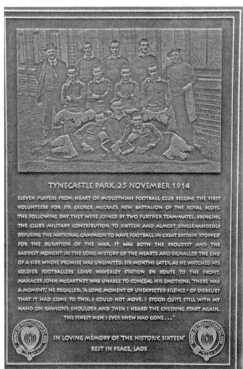

The bronze plaque which adorns the Main Stand at Tynecastle.

The Thiepval Memorial to the Missing of the Somme battlefields. It bears 72,194 names, of whom over 90 per cent died in the battles of the Somme between July and November 1916.

entire Heart of Midlothian first team, who were football league leaders when they enlisted in November 1914, prompting many others to do so. The battalion, raised by Lieutenant-Colonel Sir George McCrae, reached the farthest of any allied units on the first day of the battle, entering the tiny village of Contalmaison, deep inside the German trench system on 1 July. Three Hearts players were among the 600 members of 'McCrae's Own' killed on the opening day, and more than half the team never made it back to the Gorgie club. Yesterday, in what campaigners have described as 'unfinished business', a cairn was unveiled in a ceremony in Contalmaison, thanks largely to the Hearts Great War Memorial Appeal, which spent the last year raising the required amount of money to erect the memorial.

On Friday 27 September 2013 a bronze plaque, which was designed by Jack Alexander, was unveiled at Tynecastle in a moving ceremony. The plaque, which was gifted to the club by members of McCrae's Battalion Trust with the commission being made possible through the financial support of Jambos Kickback, shows the image of the players who enlisted for the Great War.

The ceremony was the first of a series of events to mark the centenary of the war and to recognise the lead given by the Hearts players while also acknowledging the role played by Hearts supporters and shareholders alongside comrades from Raith Rovers, Falkirk, Hibernian and other clubs.

On 16 April 2014 I received a phone call from a very good friend of mine, Alan Rae, the former Hearts physio. Alan was the bearer of good tidings. He informed me that after months of uncertainty the club would be coming out of administration and would be saved from the dreaded liquidation which had hovered around Tynecastle for many months. A famous football club had been pulled back from death's door and the name Heart of Midlothian would continue in Scottish football. Once again, the fans had played their part.

How fitting it was that this good news was received in the months leading up to the 100 anniversary of the outbreak of the Great War. What better tribute could be paid to the people back then who had made many sacrifices to ensure the club's fortunes? Who would have thought that 100 years later the followers of Hearts would be asked to make similiar sacrifices to keep the club's heart beating, and what better tribute could be paid to the men from the Heart of Midlothian who had fought and died for their country?

> Sing Hearts of Glory
> Dawn and sunset
> Hearts of Glory
> Lest we forget
> Young Scottish soldiers
> And soldiers unknown
> Who gave hearts of glory.

YOU WILL NEVER BE FORGOTTEN.

Above: From left to right, David Speed representing Heart of Midlothian, Tom Wright representing Hibernian, the author, Marshall Bowman representing Raith Rovers and John Robertson photographed at Contalmaison, 1 July 2014.

Left: From left to right, David Speed, John Robertson and the author at the Contalmaison war memorial, 1 July 2014.

John Robertson at the Arras war memorial where John Allan, the last Hearts player to be killed in action, is commemorated.

John Robertson laying a wreath at the Contalmaison Cairn on behalf of the McCrae's Battalion Trust, 1 July 2014.

Notes

1 Alexander, Jack, *McCrae's Battalion* (Edinburgh, 2004), Appendix 5.

2 *Ibid.*, p. 60.

3 For a full account of McCartney's career, see Alexander, pp. 61–72.

4 Heart of Midlothian FC, Minute Book No. 5 – March 1914 to February 1919.

5 For a detailed account of the 1914 'Football Controversy', see Alexander, pp. 13–27.

6 Alexander, p. 72.

7 The full circumstances surrounding the players' enlistment are examined in *Ibid.*, pp. 73–6

8 *Ibid.*

9 Heart of Midlothian FC, Directors' Report to Annual General Meeting of Shareholders, 6 July 1915.

10 Alexander.

11 *Ibid.*

12 Heart of Midlothian FC, Directors' Invitation card.

13 For a full account of the difficulties encountered in combining professional football with military training, see Alexander, pp. 95–100.

14 *Ibid.*

15 Heart of Midlothian FC boardroom minutes, 23 February 1915 and 1 June 1915.

16 *Ibid.*

17 Heart of Midlothian FC boardroom minutes, 6 April 1915.

18 *Ibid.*

19 Alexander, p. 99.

20 *Edinburgh Evening News.*

21 Alexander, p. 105.

22 Heart of Midlothian FC, Directors' Report to Annual General Meeting of Shareholders, 6 July 1915.

23 Alexander, p. 113.

24 *Liverpool Football Echo.*

25 Heart of Midlothian FC, Minute Book No. 5 – March 1914 to February 1919.

26 McCartney, John, *The Hearts and the Great War* (Edinburgh 1918).

27 *Edinburgh Evening News.*

28 Heart of Midlothian FC boardroom minutes, 3 April 1916.

29 Alexander, p. 123.

30 *Ibid.*, pp. 127–9.

31 *Ibid.*, p. 129.

32 *Ibid.*, p. 148.

33 For a full account of the attack of 16th Royal Scots on 1 July 1916, see *Ibid.*, pp. 155–78.

34 Heart of Midlothian FC, Minute Book No. 5 – March 1914 to February 1919.

35 For evidence of the problems faced by McCartney at this time, see Heart of Midlothian FC boardroom minutes 1916–17.

36 Heart of Midlothian FC boardroom minutes, October 1917.

37 Heart of Midlothian FC, Minute Book No. 5 – March 1914 to February 1919.

38 Heart of Midlothian FC, Directors' Report to Annual General Meeting of Shareholders, 10 June 1918.

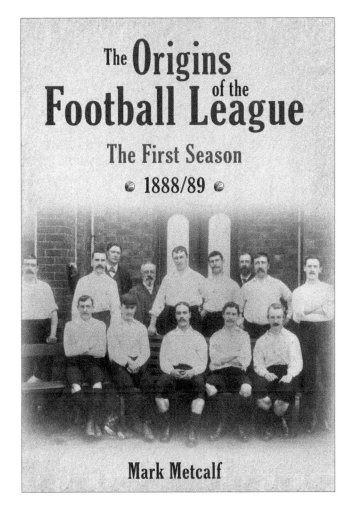

The Origins of the Football League

Mark Metcalf

'*A valuable and timely record of the birth of one of football's most important institutions.*' WHEN SATURDAY COMES

For the first time, the history of the Football League's first season is told in great depth, with reports on every match and profiles of all those who played.

978 1 4456 1881 4

224 pages, including 32 images

Available from all good bookshops or order direct from our website www.amberleybooks.com

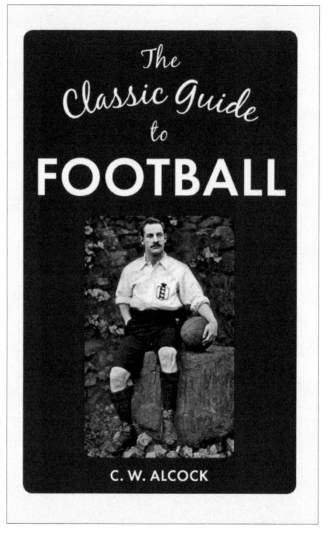

The Classic Guide to Football

C. W. Alcock

A fascinating insight into football in the 1900s and the formation
of the beautiful game by C. W. Alcock, Secretary of the Football
Association in 1871.

978 1 4456 4016 9=7
160 pages, hardback

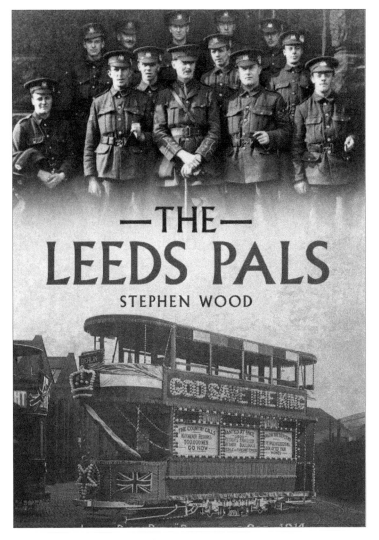

The Leeds Pals

Stephen Wood

The story of the Leeds volunteers who went to war in September
1914, following Lord Kitchener's call to arms and who went over
the top on the first day of the Battle of the Somme.

978 1 4456 1945 3
96 pages, full colour

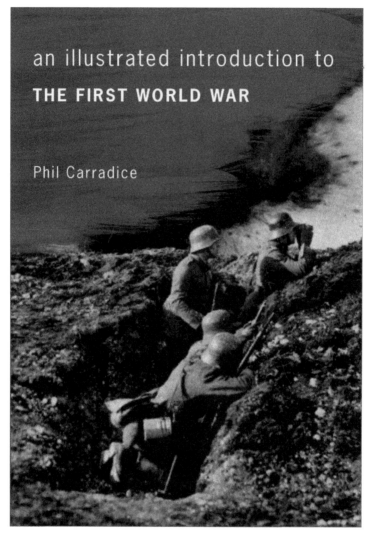